The Next Step

Finding Your *Where* In The Call *To Go*

Joshua Mead

For my wife and partner in ministry, Julie. You are not only an answer to prayer, you are my heart's desire.

Special thanks to Mrs. Jerrie Homan for the many hours she spent checking and correcting the grammar of the book text.

Preface

"Why would you go to the mission field when there are so many needs at home?"

Almost anyone who has responded to the call to ministry has either had this question posed to them or has seriously pondered it themselves. The big questions in the call to go are most often "Where do I go? Where will I serve? Should I go to the mission field or stay and serve at home? How do I discover where I am to serve when there are needs everywhere?"

The current generation of young people entering ministry have a sincere desire to be gospel-centered in their approach to ministry. Yet in this generation, we are sending fewer missionaries to the foreign field than in the previous generations. The church is called to take the gospel to the uttermost, to preach the gospel to every creature. Has God ceased to call laborers? Is the church no longer sending laborers? Or does the problem lie at the feet of those who are called?

I believe that at the heart of the labor shortage is a misconception of the biblical call to ministry. I believe that the reason few are willing to go abroad is because they who are called to ministry are not considering the implications and imperatives of what it means to be separated unto the gospel. Those who are separated to the gospel are dedicated, as Christ was, to fulfill the will and work of the Father.

As a general rule, gospel ministry should not be *need* driven. Gospel ministry is to be driven by a *passion to fulfill* the Great Commission, which is the will and work of the Father. When choosing the *where* of service, we should be motivated by the will of the Father, not necessarily the needs in a particular place. Needs are everywhere. Put your finger anywhere on a map and you can assume that there is a need there. I am sure if you are seeking a place to serve based on the need, any pastor or missionary in any state or country will provide you a lengthy list of needs you could fulfill in their location.

If we are going to fulfill the Great Commission, we must begin by understanding what the imperative is: we are commanded to go make disciples of every nation. If the imperative is to make disciples of every nation (people groups) the implication therefore is that we who are called to ministry must be going where there are no disciples. We must

2

be consumed with a passion to make Christ known where He is not named. When obedience to the last command of Christ becomes the first step in choosing where we go, I believe there will be a revival in the missionary work force.

Throughout Scripture and in the life of the early church obedience to Christ's command was the primary concern. Needs were met as a result of the fulfillment of the Great Commission. As we will study in more detail later in the book, the planting of gospel-preaching local churches is the greatest solution to the true need of mankind. The first love of the early church must become our first love—that the earth be filled with His glory (Psalm 72:19).

This was the passion of Jesus. He was consumed with zeal for the glory of His Father. Christ came to do the Father's will and to bring Him glory. Jesus told His disciples that His "meat was to do the will of Him that sent me, and to finish His work" (John 4:34). Near the end of His earthly ministry, Christ prayed triumphantly "I have glorified Thee on the earth: I have finished the work which Thou gavest me to do."

Jesus came to earth on a mission. His mission was twofold. In John 12:32, Jesus states, "And I, if I be lifted up from the earth will draw all men unto me." Jesus came to earth to die for the sins of all men. This He accomplished as He bore our sin debt, suffering the full judgement of the wrath of God on the cross, fulfilling the will of the Father. When we put our faith in Christ, we not only are born-again, we identify with His death and resurrection. In fact, Paul told us that we are crucified with Christ (Galatians 2:20). We are called to lift up the cross of Christ, to preach Christ and Christ crucified, the only means of salvation.

Jesus also stated that His death would "draw all men unto Himself." The second part of Christ's twofold mission was to draw all men to Himself. Jesus declared in John 10:16-17, "And other sheep I have, which are not of this fold: them also I must bring, and they shall hear my voice; and there shall be one fold, *and* one shepherd. Therefore doth my Father love me, because I lay down my life, that I might take it again." Jesus came for the lost sheep of the house of Israel (Matthew 15:24) but the Father's plan would prove to be much larger in scope. Jesus was sent because God so loved the world! The death of Christ made a way for the Gentile nations to come to God. The mission of drawing all men unto Christ is a mission unfinished—a task that is still being carried out by the church today. This is the mission of the church. We have been commissioned by the authority of Christ to go into all the world and preach the gospel to every creature.

4

By the time Jesus ascended to Heaven, the gospel was still contained to one location: Israel. The disciples understood the imperative to go but did not fully understand how they would carry out the mission. In Acts 1, Jesus instructs His disciples to not depart from Jerusalem but wait for the promise of the Father. A major paradigm shift was about to take place in the way God operated in the world. The temple veil was torn, and the followers of Christ would receive the indwelling Spirit. As Jews, the disciples naturally asked if the kingdom was to be restored to Israel at that time (Acts 1:6). In other words, they wanted to know if they were to fulfill mission by ruling from Jerusalem as Christ promised (Matthew 19:28).

Jesus reveals to them that mission would not be carried out by the nation of Israel and is no longer to be centralized around the temple at Jerusalem. Rather, they would receive power, after that the Holy Ghost had come upon them and they were to be witnesses unto Him in *both* Jerusalem and in all Judea and in Samaria and unto the *uttermost* part of the earth (Acts 1:8). They knew they were called to make disciples. They had not yet grasped the implication of the calling—to go make disciples where the lost are located.

Acts 1:8 is not an individual mandate. It is not even a command. Acts 1:8 is a revelation of the progression of the fulfillment of the Great Commission by the church. The Great Commission is a reorganization of operation. God's plan is to spread the message of the gospel by scattering the church, His Spirit-empowered witnesses, planting pockets of believers among all people groups. The church made up of individual believers is the temple of God. Mission through the local church is no longer centralized to the Temple in Jerusalem, as it was for the nation of Israel. The church is to be a witness among the nations, not just to the nations. If the imperative is to go make disciples of every nation, Jesus tells us that the implication is to go until the uttermost is reached.

So where is the uttermost? The uttermost is where Christ is not known. In this book, we will discover that the church is to be actively engaged in reaching the uttermost. The uttermost today is not so much a geographical location as it is the condition of a given place. To the Chinese believer, the United States is the uttermost (strictly geographically speaking). While there are certainly far less people who have access to the gospel in China than North America, not everyone is called to go to the foreign field. Jesus does not expect everyone to go. He does expect us to actively engage our uttermost. Your next-door neighbor may have never had the gospel clearly presented to him in his lifetime. He is your uttermost. You may live in an area where large segments of immigrants are moving to. They are possibly coming from restricted access nations and have never heard the gospel. They are your uttermost. Every Christian is a witness and must be seeking to evangelize those who have never heard the gospel.

While we are all called to be witnesses, this book is written primarily to those who feel they are being called into full-time Christian service. Finding your *where* in the call *to go* is usually the number one concern of those called to ministry. Today, as in the early days of the church, it seems as if the gospel has been contained to a few locations. North America, parts of Asia and Latin America are saturated with the gospel and gospel preachers. But what of the unreached nations throughout the 10/40 window? Who is called to go there? If we would begin with the Great Commission, we will discover that considering the uttermost, where Christ is not named, should and must be our priority when choosing *where* to serve.

If you have sensed the call of God to ministry and do not know where to serve, consider going where very few are ministering. If you are called to preach then you are obligated by Christ to consider going where there are no preachers. It is my sincere prayer that this book will challenge you to evaluate the imperative of your calling in light of the implications of the Great Commission. May the command to make Christ known in the uttermost part of the earth become your primary objective, until the whole earth be filled with His glory.

Joshua D. Mead

Missionary to Senegal

Afraid? Of What?

The poem, entitled "Afraid? Of What?" was written by E.H. Hamilton following the martyrdom of one of his colleagues, J.W. Vinson, at the hands of rebel soldiers in China. A young Chinese girl who escaped from the rebels related the incident that provided the inspiration for Hamilton's poem.

"Are you afraid?" the rebels asked Vinson as they ominously waved a gun in front of him.

"No," he replied with complete assurance. "If you shoot, I go straight to heaven."

His decapitated body was found later.

Afraid? Of what?
To feel the spirit's glad release?
To pass from pain to perfect peace,
The strife and strain of life to cease?
Afraid? Of that?

Afraid? Of what?
A flash – a crash – a pierced heart;
Brief darkness – Light – O Heaven's art!
A wound of His a counterpart!
Afraid? Of that?

Afraid? Of what?
To do by death what life could not –
Baptize with blood a stony plot,
Till souls shall blossom from the spot?
Afraid? Of that?

PART ONE: The First Step

Separated unto the gospel of God...now what?

---

*"Whatever you want me to do, I'll do;
where you want me to go, I'll go. I'm
yours, Lord."*

A prayer like this may not seem very significant coming from a twelve-year-old boy, but in terms of setting the course of the direction of my life, it was momentous. I don't remember who was preaching on that humid Michigan night, and I cannot recall even what was being preached. What I do remember clearly is the decision I made and the prayer I poured out to the Lord. As a twelve-year-old boy at a Christian Bible camp, responding to the Holy Spirit's prompting in my heart, I surrendered my life and my future to the will of God. That evening I died to self, offering my all for the service of the Lord. Dying is not an easy process. It is necessary, however, if you are going to be used by God. I could not even begin to imagine the life into which this death would lead me.

In I Corinthians 15:31 Paul makes an unusual statement. He emphatically declares, "I protest by your rejoicing which I have in Christ Jesus our Lord, *I die daily* (emphasis mine)." Here Paul describes a life separated unto the service of Jesus Christ as "always bearing about the dying of the Lord Jesus in the body, so that the life of Jesus also might be revealed in our body" (II Corinthians 4:10). God has a specific design and a determined purpose for each life, and He bestows upon us great honor and privilege when He counts us faithful, putting us into the ministry.

The Bible clearly teaches that a believer who is called to gospel ministry has so been chosen from his mother's womb. Psalm 22:10 says, "I was cast upon thee from the womb: thou art my God from my mother's belly." And again in Jeremiah 1:5 we read, "Before I formed thee in the belly I knew thee; and before thou camest forth out of the womb I sanctified thee, and I ordained thee a prophet unto the nations." However, God often does not make known his calling until two major events have taken place in our lives. The first event, of course, is salvation. God calls us to repent and believe in Christ by faith, as I did when I put my faith in Christ at the age of seven.

The second event that must take place for God to confirm His calling to gospel ministry is what we often term *surrender.* Only when we have been born again and have surrendered our lives completely to God's will does the Spirit reveal whether a believer has been separated unto gospel ministry. Sometimes God calls a person into full-time ministry at the moment of surrender. Others may surrender to God's will but later struggle with surrender to the details of His plan for their lives. We may know what God wants from us, but resist His calling. Whatever your experience may be, in order for God to reveal His calling upon your life, you must be brought to a moment of absolute surrender to the will of God. Throughout Scripture, a biblical pattern emerges concerning how God works in our lives. The apparent divine order of God's calling is salvation, surrender, and separation.

God-called men throughout the scripture passed through the same process. For example, the Apostle Paul recognized that God's calling in his life was established before his birth. He wrote to the Galatian church, saying, "(I)t pleased God, *who separated me from my mother's womb*, and called me by his grace, to reveal his Son in me, that I might preach him among the heathen" (Galatians 1:5-6, emphasis mine). He was on the road to Damascus, with letters of authority in hand to arrest the disciples living there. Instead, the blinding light of the presence of Christ arrested his attention. He fell to his knees, knowing the One standing before him on the road was

13

the One who had been convicting his heart. Luke records the encounter in Acts 9:5-6: "It is hard for thee to kick against the pricks," Christ declared. In that moment, Paul was gloriously saved. In that moment he surrendered his life to Christ: "Lord, what wilt thou have me to do?"

The details of Paul's calling into gospel ministry was later revealed to him through the ministry of a reluctant disciple named Ananias: "(H)e is a chosen vessel unto me, to bear my name before the Gentiles, and kings, and the children of Israel: For I will shew him how great things he must suffer for my name's sake" (Acts 9:15-16). It is interesting to note that Paul was not called to a place, but rather to bear the name of Christ to people groups: Gentiles, and kings, and the children of Israel. He was called to suffer for His name's sake. The call of God to gospel ministry is primarily a call to a life separated unto Christ to be used where and how He sees fit.

When Andrew began to follow Jesus, he "first findeth his own brother Simon, and saith unto him, We have found the Messias, which is, being interpreted, the Christ" (John 1:41). Peter believed the words of Christ and became His disciple. But the Lord had a specific plan for Peter. The Galilean fisherman did not know it when he first met Christ, but he was destined to become a fisher of men. However, before Jesus called him to apostleship, Peter had to surrender

14

his stubborn self-will. When Jesus came to Peter in Luke 5, He requested access to his boat. Peter willingly surrendered his boat to the Lord. This kind of surrender wasn't hard to do. He wasn't using it at the moment, and he was glad to see the Lord put it to good use. Every believer must be willing to surrender to the Lord the tools and gifts with which He has blessed us.

Jesus wanted more than Peter's boat that day. He wanted Peter. After speaking to the crowd, Jesus turned to Peter, instructing him to "launch out into the deep and let down your nets for a draught." This was the moment of decision for Peter. He had been more than willing to surrender the use of his boat temporarily for an impromptu preaching service. But what did this carpenter's son know about fishing? Everything within Peter told him that what Jesus was asking would end only in disappointment. Since they had failed to bring in fish during the night, fish certainly would not be around in the daytime. Luke records Peter's response, and, in doing so, gives us a glimpse of the moment of Peter's surrender of his will to the Lord's. Luke 5:5 says, "And Simon answering said unto him, Master, we have toiled all the night, and have taken nothing: nevertheless at thy word I will let down the net."

Nevertheless. This is the keyword to surrender. "I may feel this way about it, Lord; but if You command it—if You ask it of me—I will do it. I surrender my will to Yours. I surrender what I think is best to Your perfect will. If You ask it of me, Lord, I will do it." This is surrender. After the miraculous draught, the Lord revealed His calling to Peter: "(F)ear not; from henceforth thou shalt catch men. And when they had brought their ships to land, they forsook all, and followed him" (Luke 5:10-11).

Our salvation is an immutable act of God. We cannot lose our salvation. Even our separation unto gospel ministry is unchanging, unless we disqualify ourselves. Romans 11:29 tells us that "the gifts and calling of God are without repentance." While a preacher can disqualify himself from a position of service, he cannot wake up one morning and decide that he is no longer called. Paul wrote concerning his calling to preach: "(N)ecessity is laid upon me; yea, woe is unto me, if I preach not the gospel!" The call to preach is not an occupation you enter into. It is a part of who you are.

On the other hand, surrender is an ongoing process. Paul did not say that he was saved daily or that he was separated daily. He said he died daily. The only effective Christian is a dead Christian. Not physically, of course, but spiritually dead to self.

16

Thirteen Years Old and Not a Clue

Less than a year after my surrender to God's will at Bible Camp, I found myself traveling to Mexico with my pastor, who also happened to be my grandfather. Our church made a yearly missions trip to help a veteran missionary build church buildings on scattered islands just off the coast of the Gulf of Mexico. I was thirteen, had no clue how to build anything, and was mostly in the way of the grownups. I was there for the adventure and excitement of going to another country. I spent my time wandering around the island, playing with local children, and chasing wild dogs.

But the experience turned out to be life-changing. The missionary had a large trailer in which we would transport all of the tools and building supplies for the church buildings. Because of the limited space inside his van, a few of us had to travel with the equipment inside the trailer, which had no windows and was quite stuffy. At one point, the vehicle pulling the trailer stopped abruptly, and we heard muffled but stern voices speaking outside the trailer. The doors suddenly were flung open, and we were instructed to exit slowly. As my eyes adjusted to the bright sunlight, I saw a vehicle with armed soldiers seated in the back and what appeared to be the officer in charge barking orders in front of us. With machine gun in hand, the commanding officer lined us up against the side of the trailer and his soldiers proceeded to frisk us. Needless to say, I was at the same time both terrified and excited, thinking to myself what a cool story this was going to be when I returned home...if I returned home.

The trip was exciting, and the new experiences were at times overwhelming. But as a thirteen-year-old, I was certainly not contemplating what I was going to do with the rest of my life. The thought had never crossed my mind that God wanted me to do mission work—until the final day of the trip.

We loaded the van to return home and gathered one last time to say goodbye to the missionary and his family. As we stood together on his front porch, we sang a couple hymns, the missionary gave a short devotional, and then we prayed. As I bowed my head, a flood of emotion swept into my heart, and like a bolt of lightning this thought flashed into my mind: *This is what I'm going to do with the rest of my life.*

In that instant I knew that God wanted me to be a missionary. My heart began to beat faster. Tears welled up in my eyes, and I began breathing deeply, as if I had just finished running a marathon. The joy I felt in that moment is something I cannot describe, something to which only those who have received God's call can relate. I took my place in the van, and as the missionary's home faded behind us, a song began to play on my Sony Walkman (if you grew up in the 90s, you know what that is!) which was entitled "Crucified with Christ." The words are based on Galatians 2:20.

As I hear the Savior calling for daily dying,
I will bow beneath the weight of Calvary
Let my hands surrender to his piercing purpose
That holds me to the cross, yet sets me free
I will glory in the power of the cross
The things I thought were gain, I count as loss
And with his suffering I identify
And by his resurrection power I am alive!

For I am crucified with Christ
And yet I live
Not I but Christ who lives within me
The cross will never ask for more
Than I can give
For it's not my strength but His
There's no greater sacrifice
For I am crucified with Christ
And yet I live.

19

Once again, I was reminded that my life was not my own. I was surrendered to God's will, and He had now revealed to me that I was separated unto the gospel ministry. I was called to missions. I was and I am crucified with Christ. My life is not my own. "(T)he life which I now live I live by the faith of the Son of God, who loved me and gave himself for me" (Galatians 2:20). I was called to be a missionary!

Destinations and Preparations

I immediately knew where I was going to serve: somewhere in the jungles of Africa. Maybe it was from watching too many Discovery Channel documentaries as a child, but I had always dreamed of becoming an explorer in the deepest jungles of Africa. For this reason, I have never understood the fear people expressed at the thought of surrendering to missions. I've heard a lot of mission conference speakers say, "Surrendering to missions doesn't mean God is going to send you to deepest, darkest Africa." I always thought to myself, "What's wrong with that?" Africa was going to be a great adventure!

In my experience, the biggest decisions of my life seemed to simply fall into place. At age fifteen, I asked my pastor which Bible college he recommended for a young man preparing for the mission field. He recommended FaithWay Baptist College of Canada. My family and I made a visit to the college to scope it out. We happened to visit the same week that they held their annual missions conference. During the first evening service, I knew in my heart that this college was where

> Surrender your *right now*, and he will faithfully guide you to your *tomorrow*.

God wanted me to attend. God confirmed to me which country I would serve in during my freshman year at college. I even knew whom I was going to marry before we met in person! More on that later.

God does not always work in this way. Sometimes we struggle with knowing what is the right step to take. Confidence in God's calling does not necessarily mean that every detail of your calling will be easily discerned. There is one thing of which you can be sure: the God who called you and separated you unto His service is the same God who is actively guiding you to your destination. You may not know where you will end up 10, 20 or 30 years from now. You may not even know where you'll end up a year from now. But you can be assured that God has the destination of your life under control. Knowing your ministry destination is not so important as is knowing that God is preparing you right now for the journey ahead.

Proverbs 16:3 says, "Commit thy works unto the Lord and thy thoughts shall be established." To be led of God, the Christian must surrender his every moment to God. We must surrender daily to His leading and His working in our lives. Take every opportunity to let God mold you—wherever you may find yourself. Surrender your *right now,* and he will faithfully guide you to your *tomorrow.*

I tried to take advantage of every relevant opportunity to better prepare myself for the mission field. I read several missionary biographies. My parents gave me a copy of the Jim Elliot story. He and the team of five missionaries inspired me, and I began taking flight lessons to become a bush pilot. After ten hours of flight time, I ran out of money and decided not to pursue it further.

While I was still in high school, my youth group and my school would usually produce a yearly missions drama. I played the roles of both Jim Elliot and John Stam in reader's theaters. My mom asked me to stop playing the role of missionary martyrs!

At one point, I read the story of how Hudson Taylor would purposely give away his work salary while still living in England. He wanted to prove God and grow his faith in the Lord's promise to provide. He reasoned that if he didn't have faith for God to provide for him in England, how could he have faith in China? I decided to follow his example. I began giving over half of my salary to our church missions program. I had a large sum of money saved for college. Days before departing to college, I put half of it in the offering at my home church. I wanted to see God meet my need. When we arrived at the American/Canadian border and exchanged the money, we found out that the American dollar was worth a significant amount more than the Canadian dollar. The Canadian dollar amount that we received was just about enough to pay the entire school year!

One of the first messages I heard preached at college was on Malachi 3 entitled "Prove the Lord." I had a few hundred dollars to take care of personal needs, such as laundry, gas for my car, and Tim Horton's coffee. (Remember, I went to college in Canada where money for Tim Horton's is a necessity.) Being a foreigner, I was restricted to working on campus where my salary went directly to my school bill. I had no way of making an income to meet my needs. If I gave the extra cash I had on hand to the Lord, He would have to take care of my needs. I wanted to take God up on His challenge in Malachi. I used the money to pay for some of the suits used for the college traveling singing group. The rest I placed in the offering, trusting God to meet my needs.

Within a couple weeks I needed money for laundry. Afraid I would receive demerits for the mountain of clothes piling up on my bed, I asked God to provide a little bit of cash so that I could go the laundromat. Shortly thereafter, a roommate approached me and asked me to do his laundry for him. His boss had increased his hours at work, and he had no time to go to the laundromat himself. I told him I'd be glad to do it for him. He handed me $15, instructing, "Here is money for my laundry, some money for gas, and a little extra to do your own laundry if you want. Maybe get a Tim Horton's coffee with the spare change." (I don't think he actually said that last sentence, but I was thinking it.) I probably stared at the money as if he were offering me one million dollars, and he might as well have been. God had provided my need!

Time and time again, the Lord provided cash when I needed it—and often in the most unusual ways. I needed money for a haircut and new shoes for work. Another college student approached me and handed me $50, telling me that the Lord put it on his heart to give it to me. He said that I should use it to get a haircut and buy a pair of shoes. He could probably see my need for a haircut, but I hadn't told anyone my need for new shoes for work! By the end of the year, I had extra money on my school bill. God has proved Himself faithful time and again. Truly "my God shall supply all your need according to his riches in glory by Christ Jesus" (Philippians 4:19).

While I was still in high school, my youth pastor gave me some great advice. He encouraged me to begin praying for my college roommate. He told me to pray that God would give me a roommate who would challenge my spiritual growth, which I began doing faithfully. I saw the wisdom of his advice come to fruition the first week of college. It was an exciting and awkward time of adjusting to the new life of being a freshman. Rather than one or two roommates, I actually had around ten! A sophomore named Rick befriended me after literally beating me in a game of knuckles: a game where two people try to bash each other's knuckles until one or the other gives up. We bonded over this silly game and began a friendship that would ultimately influence my decision for choosing Senegal.

Afraid? Of What?

I shared my desire to be a missionary in Africa and Rick shared his desire to serve in a place where there were few churches—a pioneer mission field. I gave him a copy of a message I had listened to several times during high school. It was given by the late Darrell Champlin entitled "Afraid? of

What?" In the message, the great missionary statesman called for a new generation of an old generation reborn. He urged the necessity of having a pioneer spirit—a spirit that seemed to be lacking among the youth of today. We began praying that God would give us a pioneering spirit. We prayed that God would send us to preach the gospel to those who have never heard.

We discovered an important Biblical principle concerning the will of God. In Psalm 37:4 David penned, "Delight thyself also in the Lord, and He shall give thee the desires of thine heart." If we would delight in the Lord, He would give us the desires of our heart. We learned that when we delighted in God, our desires would align with His. He would put His desires on our hearts. To know God's will we must know God. In verse 5 of the same Psalm we read, "Commit thy way unto the Lord, trust also in Him; and He shall bring it to pass." We decided on three specific desires that we wanted to commit to the Lord. The first was that God would lead us to a pioneer-type field. The second desire was that God would allow us to work as a team. The third desire— one that God fulfilled beyond what I could imagine—was that God would give us pretty wives!

We had the calling, the drive, and the passion to go but did not as yet have a place to go. How does one go about making the decision of where to go? Was there a specific process we had to follow in order to discover where God wanted us? We prayed the prayer of David in Psalm 143:10: "Teach me to do thy will; for thou art my God: Thy spirit is good; lead me in the land of uprightness." We knew what we wanted to do but did not know where we were going to go. Afraid? Of What? We were ready to go!

Mine Eye Affecteth My Heart

Most men enrolled in Bible college as theology majors do not struggle with whether they are called to preach. Many students entering Bible college have already surrendered to full-time Christian service. The struggle for most ministry students is figuring out *where* God wants them to serve. As a young man with my whole life of ministry ahead of me, I knew what I wanted to do. I simply didn't know where I would serve or where to begin. I wanted to know how missionaries made their decisions when choosing their country of service.

As a rule, most people make major life decisions based on what they know in their heart is the right choice for them. A believer who is sensitive to the Spirit of God will be assured in his heart of God's leading. When you delight yourself in the Lord, He gives you the desires of your heart to help guide the direction of your life.

However, Scripture reveals to us another life principle in Lamentations 3:51, "Mine eye affecteth my heart." Most men and women called into full-time ministry—especially those who have a heart for missions—choose their country based on the need that they see in that country. This is why mission conferences are so important. When young people are exposed to the reality of the need for laborers in the far corners of the world, what they see will influence and affect their hearts, which in turn is instrumental in finalizing a decision to serve on a particular field. Who hasn't seen a missionary presentation and not been burdened to leave everything and go to that field? It is normal Christian compassion to see people without Christ and be burdened to do something about it.

Yes, there are many other factors that go into the final decision, such as the influence of a veteran missionary, the counsel of your pastor, and your personal suitability to the field. However, the fact remains that what we see has the greatest impact on what we decide to do and where we decide to go. But as we mentioned earlier, gospel service is not primarily driven by the needs we see.

Choosing a place of service based on the need you see is not necessarily a wrong way to choose a mission field or a place to pastor, but there are certain limitations it creates in the potential choices of where we could and should go. When we decide to go based solely on seeing the need of a particular field, we automatically leave out of consideration those fields that we have not been exposed to. Often the mission fields we have never heard of have the fewest missionaries. For instance, there is a good chance you have never heard of The Gambia. The reason is that, as I write this, there are only a handful of Baptist missionaries serving in that country. For this reason, we have close friends who have raised support for serving in The Gambia in almost less than a year! (Who said raising support takes forever? Go to a pioneer field and you'll have support in no time!)

Consider what happens if we only decide *where* to serve based solely on *what* we see. As we have already discussed, missionaries often choose what country to serve in based only upon the need that they have observed. More than likely, the missionary candidate has been exposed to the need by someone already in that country (a veteran missionary, for example). A question remains, namely, "Who is going to the countries or people groups that no one is reaching?" When a country or people group is unreached there are no or very few church planters representing their needs to the larger missionary workforce. If we go to a field only because we saw the need presented by a missionary in a mission conference, and it touched our heart, then we must consider what happens to the unreached parts of the world that very few people see or hear about.

> *Choosing a place of service based on the need you see is not necessarily a wrong way to choose a mission field, but there are certain limitations it creates in the potential choices of where we could and should go.*

My mission board, Baptist International Missions, Inc. has a large concentration of missionaries in Brazil, the Philippines, and Uganda. Why? Logically, it is because there is already a large presence of missionaries in Brazil, the Philippines, and Uganda. The more exposure a need receives, the more opportunity there is to respond and meet that need.

We have come to a place in our missions emphasis where we are sending missionaries to places where missionaries already are. That is not wrong. It's just not enough. I thank God that many mission agencies such as BIMI have directors who place an emphasis on opening new fields and recruiting missionaries to serve in a pioneer capacity. This emphasis will certainly help influence missionary candidates to go serve in unreached places. But the fact remains that the majority of laborers are going to countries that already have access to the gospel. As long as there are people groups who do not have access to the gospel, the Great Commission remains unfulfilled.

As a freshman in college, I knew very little about the world at large. The call to be a missionary with a pioneer spirit meant I had to look for a place that had few or no missionaries. Having a desire and formulating a plan are two very different things. When it concerns choosing a field of service, it is very difficult to envision a plan when there is no structure in place upon which you can confirm your decision.

For example, the easier decision would be to look at the need of a country like Uganda, where BIMI has approximately 16 families serving. There is truly a need for more laborers in that country. While you are considering where to serve, a missionary to Uganda visit's your church or college and presents the needs in his country. After seeing the need, you begin to envision yourself moving there to minister. To envision what your ministry would look like, you would survey the ministry structure which is already in place. Churches are being planted, orphanages for war-scarred children are being built, and radio stations and media outreach programs need partners to help expand the reach of the gospel. The need is great, and there is a structure in place that one could easily plug into with ample opportunities to serve. You go because you were motivated by what you saw and felt confident to go because of the ministry structure already in place.

But at some point, in the past, a missionary had to go there when there was nothing: no structure, no church, no outreach. Someone had a vision of what God could do where there was no ministry structure in place. While Uganda still needs laborers, there are countries and people groups across North Africa and other areas which span the 10/40 window who still have no ministry structure in place. They are countries with limited, and in some cases, restricted access to the gospel. They have no or very few churches and church planters. They are countries in need of a pioneer missionary. We just don't hear about them in North America because few are going to reach them and in turn few are reporting on their need.

Pioneer missions takes pioneer vision: the faith to see what only God can do when there is nothing but an empty mission field before you. If we only go to those countries we see or hear about, logically the places we do not see or hear about will be neglected. The uttermost remains unreached.

> *Most young men called to preach assume, "I am not called to be a missionary. God has called me to pastor."*

To Infinity and Beyond

I wanted to go to an empty field. I wanted to go to a mission field where there were few or no missionaries, where the need for gospel-preaching church planters was greatest. I wanted to make the gospel accessible to people groups who had either never heard the gospel or had very little access to the gospel. But how does one discern the *where*? Turning to Scripture, my friend and I began to study the life of the Apostle Paul. We approached the book of Acts with these questions in mind: How did Paul decide which cities he would visit on his missionary journeys? What process did he employ that led him to decide where he would plant a church?

Acts 13 tells us that Paul was set apart by the Holy Spirit for a specific task. Acts 13:2 says, "As they ministered to the Lord, and fasted, the Holy Ghost said, Separate me Barnabas and Saul for the work whereunto I have called them." The local church at Antioch confirmed this calling and sent them away: "And when they had fasted and prayed, and laid their hands on them, they sent them away" (Acts 13:3). Verse 4 continues by telling us that they went, being sent by the Holy Spirit: "So they, being sent forth by the Holy Ghost, departed."

The process of figuring out 'the where' of missions seemed self-explanatory: respond to the Spirit's call, confirm the call through your local church and then go where the Spirit is leading. Allow the Holy Spirit to lead you to the place where He wants you to serve. Simple enough, right? Not exactly.

I once read that over 90% of ministers who speak English as their first language are serving in America. Considering that the U.S. population makes up only 4.4% of the world's population, at some point we need to ask ourselves what is the church in America doing wrong when it comes to figuring out the where of gospel work. Why do the majority of God-called preachers in America stay in a country that is already saturated with access to the gospel? Most young men called to preach assume, "I am not called to be a missionary. God has called me to pastor." Every young man who has sensed God's call should confront himself with these two questions: Is God's call on my life to preach an automatic calling to pastor in America, or is God's calling to preach an automatic call to go to the unreached uttermost?

By the end of this book, I want to break down the common assumptions about what it really means to be called to missions. We will discover that if we begin with the Great Commission as the basis for where God wants us to serve, rather than the assumption that a call to preach is a call to pastor in North America, I believe we will see many more laborers going to the unreached uttermost parts of the world.

I have read that less than 1% of mission dollars are allocated to the unreached people groups of the world. This is a problem, but the issue is not our giving. American churches give more money to missions and charity than any other country in the history of the world. The reason so few of those dollars go to the unreached peoples of the world is because there are so few preachers willing to go to those unreached places. 30% of Independent Baptist missionaries are serving in just 5 countries. There are over 250 countries in the world! There is such a great need, but somehow, we are not fulfilling that need.

A Bible college student who recently visited us in Senegal told me about a missionary who spoke to a group of 200 preacher boys at his school. The missionary asked the students who felt called to pastor in America to raise their hands. 188 students raised their hands! When he asked the those who felt called to missionary service to raise their hands, the remaining 12 responded. Only 6% of preacher boys at one of America's largest independent Baptist colleges are preparing for the mission field.

As my friend and I journeyed with Paul through the book of Acts, we moved from city to city as the gospel was preached and churches were planted. From the start, we recognized two aspects of Paul's church planting work. First of all, he always worked in a team, never alone. His mission team was literally a travelling church! We say 'churches plant churches' and rightly so. Paul moved from city to city with his team of Christian workers, generally leaving someone behind to oversee the growth of the young church as he and his 'nomadic church' moved on to plant more churches. Paul wasn't planting churches as an individual missionary. He was planting churches as a team—a very real, mobile body of believers.

Secondly, we noticed that Paul was going where there was no gospel witness. The heart of his mission philosophy was obedience to and the fulfillment of the Great Commission. In 2 Corinthians 10:14-16, he told the church, "For we stretch not ourselves beyond our measure, as though we reached not unto you: for we are come as far as to you also in preaching the gospel of Christ: Not boasting of things without our measure, that is, of other men's labours; but having hope, *when your faith is increased*, that we shall be enlarged by you according to our rule abundantly, *To preach the gospel in the regions beyond you*, and not to boast in another man's line of things made ready to our hand" (emphasis mine).

Paul always had his sights set on the regions beyond. Even while he was planting a church in one city, his heart was burdened for the next where there was no gospel witness. His motivation to obey the Great Commission was the driven by a passion to see God's glory spread throughout the earth. This was the key to Paul choosing the *where* of his strategic church planting.

If Jesus commanded believers to go into all the world and preach the gospel to every creature, then the first question a young man called to preach should consider is "Where in the world are there no preachers?" followed by "I'll go there."

When we came to Acts 16, we discovered an open secret to Paul's process of decision making. We learned how Paul chose the cities where he would minister. We discovered why God was able to use him so mightily. What we found surprised us. Paul was not, primarily, motivated by the needs of the lost. Most messages that are preached from this passage emphasize the *need* of the unreached as the overarching motivation for going. They emphasize the Macedonian vision and the cry of the lost for help. "Come over and help us," we hear the lost crying as they grope in the darkness seeking truth, waiting for the missionary to fly in with the glorious message of salvation.

This may sound like a noble motivation for going, but there is a weakness inherent to it. We emphasize the need of the lost as a motivation for going to reach them, but once we reach the field we find out that the majority of unbelievers are not interested in the gospel. Many of the unreached places of the world are actually hostile to the gospel. We become disillusioned to our very purpose for being there; and when we see little to no results, we pack up and head home, assuming we have either failed or misinterpreted God's calling. Some say that over 50% of missionaries who make it to the field do not return for a second term. That number may actually be higher.

As a freshman in college, I knew I wanted to go to a place where there were few or no missionaries, and I wanted to work on a team, like the Apostle Paul. I did not know where that would be specifically. Did I have to wait for some sort of a call for help like the Macedonian vision? If you are waiting for the unreached Muslims, Hindus, and Buddhists of the world to call you up and plead with you to come and plant a church among them, you'll be waiting a long time.

Taking a closer look at Acts 16, we soon discovered what appeared to be Paul's motive and process for choosing where he would go to preach the gospel.

"Now when they had gone throughout Phrygia and the region of Galatia, and were forbidden of the Holy Ghost to preach the word in Asia, After they were come to Mysia, they assayed to go into Bithynia: but the Spirit suffered them not. And they passing by

Mysia came down to Troas. And a vision appeared to Paul in the night; There stood a man of Macedonia, and prayed him, saying, Come over into Macedonia, and help us. And after he had seen the vision, immediately we endeavoured to go into Macedonia, assuredly gathering that the Lord had called us for to preach the gospel unto them" (Act 16:6-10).

As we took a closer look at the passage, something odd stood out to us. Luke tells us that Paul wanted to go into Asia, but he was stopped. Then he tried to go into Bithynia, and again he was hindered. In both instances, it was the Holy Spirit stopping him! The first questions I asked myself were "Who is leading Paul in his decision-making process? Is it the Holy Spirit?" The immediate answer to the second question, in the context of this passage, is no, not really. So, what is driving Paul to go to Asia and Bithynia? Is he being carnal and trying to do his own thing? Again, I would say no. It was definitely not carnality that gave Paul the desire to take the gospel to an unreached region where he would most likely be met with intense persecution and opposition. The answer came to me when a missionary shared an illustration in a college class during a mission conference.

Just Pick a Place and Go!

A veteran missionary shared his testimony in our missions' class. He closed by asking a series of questions and giving us an illustration. The missionary asked us, "Do you want to know God's will for your life? Do you want to discover where God will have your serve?" I sat forward in my seat, listening intently. Of course, I wanted to know the answer to these questions! How do you figure out the where of God's call? The missionary continued, "If you want to find out where God would have you serve, you have to simply pick a direction and go. Start moving forward." He then gave an illustration that made perfect sense, "You can't steer a car in any one particular direction until it is moving forward. Take the first step, get your car rolling forward, and God will direct you as you move. Just pick a place and go!"

That was the secret! You can't direct a car if it is sitting still. You can't sit around waiting for the lost to ask for your help. The world doesn't want your message. The world doesn't want your Jesus. The reason God revealed to Paul where the need was the greatest and where he would be most effective is that he was in constant forward motion.

The call to preach is a call to obey the Great Commission literally. Therefore, any young man who has sensed God's call to preach is obligated to base his decision concerning the *where* of his work on the Word of God, specifically the Great Commission. The first question we must consider is not the default "where in North America will I pastor" but rather where in the world are there people who have no access to the gospel. Paul basically said, "If I'm called to preach, and we are to preach to every creature, then I want to know where in the world are there no preachers. I'm going there." Because he was always in forward motion, obeying the Great Commission by seeking to go to unreached peoples, the Holy Spirit was able to direct and use Paul.

The reason we don't have more preachers in unreached places of the world is because we are simply not obeying the Bible Commission that is directly linked to the call to preach. I'm not saying that every preacher has to go overseas. What I am suggesting is that somehow we are falling short of fulfilling the Great Commission. I believe this is mostly attributed to an unintentional divorce we have created between the call to preach and the Lord's command to go.

Missions is the gospel in action. Missions is the gospel in forward motion. In Acts 8:4 the Bible tells us that "(T)hey that were scattered abroad went every where preaching the word." In this passage, the verb translated preaching is *euaggelizo* from which we derive the English word *to*

41

evangelize. The verse is literally saying the persecuted believers went everywhere *evangelizing* the word. Good news is only effective if it is being proclaimed! We have been commissioned to take the good news, the gospel, to the uttermost and evangelize every nation. We are obligated to evangelize the uttermost.

Luke records for us his purpose statement for writing the gospel that bears his name in Acts 1:1. He writes, "The former treatise have I made, O Theophilus, of all that Jesus began both to do and teach." We are to build our lives on the Lord Jesus Christ, doing what He did and living what He taught. Using this as his introduction to the Acts of the Apostles, Luke implies that the church is not only built upon the teaching and doings of our Lord, but is a continuation of what the Lord did and taught. Paul wrote Timothy and urged him to continue in the things that he had learned (2 Timothy 3:14). In John 20:21, Jesus tells His disciples, "As my Father hath sent Me, even so, send I you." We are to go and teach all nations, baptizing them in the name of the Father, the Son, and of the Holy Spirit: teaching them to observe all that the Lord commanded us. The church is to continue of the work Jesus started.

Surrendering to the uttermost should not be a fearful prospect. Not only is our mission to go a direct command from

Christ, but we have a guaranteed victory when we advance on the enemy. Jesus told his disciples in Matthew 16:24 that He would build His church, and the gates of hell shall not prevail against it. Have you ever considered why Jesus phrased it this way? Why does He say the gates of hell? The gates of a city are the last defense. We have the idea that we have victory only against Satan's attack. We can and do overcome Satan's offensive maneuvers against us, but that is not what Jesus is talking about in this passage. Christ is proclaiming that we, the church that He is building, will be on the offensive. We will advance upon Satan's territory, putting him in retreat and even his last defenses will not stand against the forward march of the Spirit-empowered church. We must be advancing on the gates of hell. It is time the church return to the offensive. We must, as C.T. Studd put it, seek to run a rescue shop within a yard of hell.

Where are the gates of hell? They stand at the border of every nation where Christ is not named. They tower over the lost masses in India; they surround the unreached villages of Africa. The gates of hell remain firmly closed in almost every Islamic nation. Jesus promised that these gates would prove futile to the advance of the church. The only reason they remain standing in defiance of the gospel is that we, the church, are not storming them with all our might!

Satan has no new defense. He uses the same tactics in every nation where false religion holds sway over the masses. During our language training in Quebec, Canada, I interviewed a Baptist preacher for a short film we produced about the history of Baptists in the French-Canadian province. He explained to me that when he was a boy, the local priest would visit their public school to speak on the Catholic religion. He distinctly remembered two things the priest told the class to avoid. First, they were told to not read the Bible. The Bible was to be interpreted by the clergy. Second, they were instructed to avoid the Protestants, especially the Baptists!

Later, in Senegal, a young man in our church who grew up a Muslim, told me that there are two things they are taught as children: Never read the Bible (because it has been corrupted by Christians) and never listen to the Christians, especially the missionaries!

The majority of those who follow these religions are often not as familiar with their own core doctrines as they are with what they are taught to not believe. This is Satan's only tactic. He will attempt to keep people from the truth at all cost. Yet this defense against truth has a weakness inherit to it. We all have a sin nature that seeks to rebel against authority. We often deal with people seeking out what the Bible teaches simply because they are curious to find out what they have been told their whole life to not read. A young man we led to the Lord invited his Quranic teacher to our Bible Center. He shared a passage from the Sermon on the Mount. As the teacher read the passage in Arabic, he paused and proclaimed, "My whole life I've been told the words of this book are a lie and are corrupt. But I have never heard such truth in my life. These are good words!" The gospel will make the walls of Satan's defense fall.

Paul was not ashamed of the gospel. He knew it was the power of God unto salvation. Armed with the Sword of the Spirit, Paul advanced upon the gates of hell and watched them fall, one city after another, as he marched triumphantly through them. He told the Corinthian church: "Now thanks be unto God, which always causeth us to triumph in Christ, and maketh manifest the savour of his knowledge by us in every place" (2 Corinthians 2:14). With a guaranteed victory, why is it that so few are willing to go? Why not just pick a place and go?

Casting Lots...or Something Like That

After class was over and the missionary finished his presentation, I found my friend, who was just as excited as I was about the car illustration. Let's just pick a place and go, we decided. We'll choose a country and make plans to go there. If God wants us there, He'll direct us and if He does not, at least we are moving forward so He can lead us. That's what the Apostle Paul did, why not us? It would be like casting lots...only not.

We also thought it would be a good idea to have a Bible verse to back up our reasoning. The car illustration was great, but it's always good to make sure that your decisions are biblically based! God led us to Proverbs 16:9. This verse says, "A man's heart deviseth his way: but the Lord directeth his steps." A heart that is already submissive to God and obedient to His Word is ready to make a plan. Verse 1 of the same chapter says, "The preparations of the heart in man, and the answer of the tongue, is from the Lord." We knew what God had been doing in our hearts and lives during the past few months. We decided that we were going to pick a place at random and make a plan to go there, letting God direct our steps.

The key to discovering the *where* in the work of God is in initiating the first step. Once you form a plan, take the first step toward the execution of that plan; and God will guide the next

With a guaranteed victory, why is it that so few are willing to go?

46

step. As you journey forward with God, you'll discover that it has been God leading you from the very start. I believe the reason God does not always make the first step clear to us is that He wants us to take the first step by faith. The first step needs to be a step of obedience to His Word and His calling, motivated by love for Him from the heart. Paul's motivation was love for Jesus, a love that drove him to extreme obedience of the Great Commission, the very heartbeat of Jesus.

Once we reached this point, we now had to decide how we would choose at random a country to serve in. It had to be a country where there were few or no missionaries. We wanted to go pioneer the gospel to an unreached region. We wanted to go where it was hard, where no preacher had gone before. Maybe we did romanticize the idea just a bit; but that did not change the fact that we knew God had called us to preach, and we wanted to go where there were no preachers.

A second requirement was that this pioneer, unreached country be in Africa. This was non-negotiable. I had known since I was five years old that I was destined to work in Africa. I always envisioned myself chopping my way through the dense jungles, fighting rain and wild animals in order to access some tribe who had never seen a white man. Little did I know that much of Africa, south of the Sahara Desert, has a great Christian influence; or at least it could be labeled as being "gospel-accessible." This is not to diminish the need in these countries. However, the 10/40 window of unreached people groups doesn't run through the jungles. It runs through the blistering desert sands of northern Africa. If we were going to pioneer the gospel in Africa, it was going to be done Lawrence of Arabia style, not David Livingstone style!

In our missions' class, the teacher gave every student a final project, worth almost half of the class grade. A hollowed-out globe filled with the names of random countries was passed around to every student. Each student would blindly choose a country and then prepare a presentation as if they were raising support to go there as a missionary. My friend and I decided that whatever country he pulled out of the globe would become the country we would serve in!

The odds of blindly picking a country that met the two aforementioned requirements were astronomical, I'm sure. But, if God was in it, He would direct our steps. In this case, He could direct our hand to choose the right country. The day of the drawing was approaching. The anticipation was building. We still hadn't told anyone of our crazy plan.

You can imagine the excitement we felt the day of the drawing. Other students were choosing their country in order to do a project to pass the class. We were there to choose a country where we might very well end up serving for the rest of our lives! I could barely contain the excitement. As the globe slowly made its way across the room, I thought about which countries might be inside it. What were the chances of our choosing at random a country in Africa that has few or no missionaries? The globe reached my desk, and I pulled out a folded piece of paper. I opened it up and read "Dominica." "Hmm," I thought to myself, "Sounds like a nice country. Maybe I'll go there when I retire."

The globe reached the desk of my friend. I honed in on his hand like a hawk seeking his prey as he slowly removed the folded slip of paper from the globe. There in his hand was my future—my destiny—the fulfillment of my calling. He unfolded it, read it, and then turned to me. My eyes widened, my heart stopped beating. "What country is it?" I whispered intensely. He looked at the paper, smiled, folded it and put it in his pocket. "Shhh," he replied, "The teacher is talking." What a loser.

As soon as class was over, I rushed over to him, knowing that in his pocket—on that piece of paper—was written my future *where*. "What country is it? Is it in Africa? Is it a pioneer country?"

He removed the paper from his shirt and said, "The country is Mauritania."

"Mauritania," I said nodding, "Sounds like a pioneer country. I've never heard of any missionaries in Mauritania. In fact, I've never heard of Mauritania."

"Me neither," he laughed, and we both ran up to the library and found an atlas.

We opened the atlas, turned to the "M" section and found Mauritania. My eyes widened and I stood speechless. There it was, located on the northwestern coast of Africa! We couldn't believe it. Surely Mauritania had to be a pioneer country. It sounded like a pioneer country. We had never met any missionaries going to Mauritania. Then I noticed two possible reasons why we had never heard of missionaries in Mauritania. The first thing I noticed was that it was located on the part of the continent of Africa where the earth was all brown. There was no green. Not for miles around. The Sahara Desert covers an area of over 3.6 million miles and stretches across north Africa from Morocco and Mauritania in the west to Egypt in the east. Who wants to go to the desert?

I also noticed the full title of the country's name: The Islamic Republic of Mauritania. The reason we hadn't heard of missionaries in this country is because it is a country under

Sharia law. It is illegal to openly evangelize; and if its citizens convert from Islam to Christianity, they can be put to death. The more we learned about this country, the more we questioned the sanity of our method of randomly choosing a country.

In order to serve in restricted access countries, one must have a special skill or job to use as a means to gain access into said country. I thank God for men and women who have specialized skills or training that allow them to enter these otherwise "closed" countries. However, at the time, my friend and I had no special skills to speak of that would allow us to enter Mauritania. We studied the atlas further and soon noticed, situated just below Mauritania, sat the country of Senegal. In northern Senegal, on the border of Mauritania, is a city called St. Louis.

> *A man's heart deviseth his way: but the Lord directeth his steps.*

We had met a missionary the previous year who was raising support to return to St. Louis. His parents had served there as pioneer missionaries for 18 years, and he was returning to continue their work. We thought Senegal would make a great access point into the north. We began to formulate a plan.

Our plan was simple: we would go to St. Louis, Senegal, and work with the missionary we had met. Making our base in northern Senegal, we would sneak into Mauritania from time to time and share the gospel until we were either exposed as missionaries and chased out, or worse, martyred. One of our plans, a plan we took very seriously at the time, was to join the Dakar Rally. The Dakar Rally was a race that began in Paris, went down through the deserts of North Africa, wound its way through Mauritania, and finally ended up in Dakar, Senegal. We would navigate the course on dirt bikes and share the gospel at checkpoints until the locals chased us away with swords. As they came after us, we would swiftly ride off into the sunset on to the next checkpoint. We'd be renegade missionaries! We had no idea what we were talking about. Looking back now it sounds foolhardy, but at least we had a plan to do something!

We devised a plan and committed it to the Lord. It was now up to God to direct our steps. If God were going to direct us, we had to make sure that we did not interfere. We decided not to disclose our plan to anyone, not to the missionary with whom we planned to work nor even to our parents. We would let God confirm our plan or redirect us as He saw fit, taking one step at a time in the direction toward Senegal. I figured that God would not confirm this plan for another few years; after all, I was still a freshman with a lot of schooling left to finish. Little did I know just how quickly God would confirm this crazy plan.

Crazy, Radical Walk-On-Water Faith

When you step back and think about it, leaving the future of your ministry to a random draw of the hat seems crazy. But that is just the thing about Biblical faith. God loves crazy, radical faith. We know that without faith it is impossible to please God. Most of us are content to believe what the Bible says about who God is and what He is capable of doing. Believing God is capable of doing great things and actually attempting to do great things for God are two very different things. How many of us are willing to do something for God that maybe He hasn't clearly asked us to do? You believe God can do the impossible. But have you never considered stepping out by faith and trying something improbable?

Consider the account of when Jesus walked on water. In Matthew 14 the disciples were crossing the sea when a storm arose. The situation quickly escalated into a violent and dangerous situation. Then Jesus comes by, casually walking on the water. We are told that the disciples saw Someone walking on the water in the middle of a storm and were afraid. They thought they were seeing a ghost. The fact that they automatically assumed it was a ghost tells me one of two things. Either seeing ghosts walk on water was a common occurrence, or their fear caused them to come to irrational

53

conclusions. I believe the latter was the case. Our fears always lead us to draw irrational conclusions which cripples us from moving forward for the Lord. Their fear blinded them from seeing the Lord and what He was capable of doing. He had just fed 5,000 men with a few fish and loaves of bread. If Jesus could accomplish that impossible feat, surely, He could walk on water.

When Christ called out to assure them that it was indeed He himself, their fears were put to rest. In other words, they believed Jesus. They believed His word. Given who Jesus was and what He was capable of, it was rational to accept by faith that He was walking on water.

It is easy to believe that Jesus was able to walk on water while seated in the safe confines of the boat. Enter Peter. As was his custom, he is about to do something crazy, something improbable—at least by human standards. He wasn't about to let the Lord to have all the fun. "Lord, if it be thou, bid me come unto thee on the water" (Matthew 14:28). How many of us have crazy, radical faith like Peter? I'm not talking about faith to believe that Jesus can do the impossible. Crazy, radical and yes, even reckless faith believes that God can and will do the improbable through you. Would you have asked the Lord, "If it's really You, and if you allow it Jesus, I'm jumping out of the boat and joining You!"

Fear will not only keep you from seeing the impossible, it will keep you from considering the improbable. Many are fearful to surrender to the Lord's will because of what they think He might ask of them. But if you can testify to the faithfulness of God to you where you are now, would you not consider that He will be faithful to you no matter what He may ask of you or where He may lead you? I saw God provide money for laundry when I was a college student in Canada with no money. Because I saw God do the impossible, I was led to venture into what was improbable: choosing a field of service by pulling a country out of a hat at random.

Notice that Jesus had not asked nor commanded Peter to join him on the water. Peter's radical faith and his identification with Jesus led him to do what had not even crossed the minds of the other disciples. Walking on water is impossible, but Jesus is God, so it was not a big deal. Jumping overboard to join Him on the water, now that is improbable. Like Peter, my friend and I came up with a crazy idea, and God blessed it: "Lord, I'm going to choose a random country out of this hat and go there. If You can do the impossible and can save people under the bondage of Islam, then I'm going to do the improbable and ask you to let me join You there!"

How many times have I heard people close to me reason with me when I was a young perspective missionary: "Why go to Africa, there is a need here in America. We need you here." I know they are well meaning. I know they give to missions and love and support missionaries who go. But when

> *When you truly trust God to do the impossible, you will consider doing what formerly seemed improbable.*

someone close to them, inside their boat, says they are jumping ship and going to walk on water (going to the foreign mission field, for example) those who are left in the boat are left scratching their heads. "Why jump out? We need you here. God could really use you as a pastor or evangelist here in America."

Peter was probably the most experienced of all the fishermen on that boat. He knew better than to jump out of the boat onto the water. But something within him told him that if Jesus could do it, so could he. Maybe he was being presumptuous. Maybe he was just exercising radial, reckless faith. Whatever the case was, Peter is the only one of the disciples who get to say they have walked on water!

Why jump out of the boat onto the water? Because Jesus is there. Because He told us to go and going should be the first consideration not the last option. We jump out because there are enough workers in the boat to keep it afloat.

We jump out of the boat and go because there is something in our heart that tells us that God has something more for us—something great and exciting and terrifying and hard—waiting for us. Going to the foreign mission field might seem as terrifying as the thought of walking on water in a storm; but if Jesus is there, then there is no better and safer place to be! When Jesus is there, we can do the impossible.

God's Precision

My friend and I would pray about our plan and discuss what life in Senegal might look like. I still had three and a half years of college left, so I did not expect God to confirm our plan immediately. He did. A few days before school let out for summer break, I called my family in the States. My mom told me that my grandmother had invited us to attend her church

> Fear will not only keep you from seeing God do the impossible, it will cripple you from considering doing the improbable.

where a missionary to Africa would be speaking. We were to share a meal at her house after the service with the missionary and his family. My family knew my desire to go to Africa, but I had not told them about Senegal. I asked my mom what country the missionary served in. She said, "Just a second, I have their prayer card here." After a short pause she replied, "They are from a country called Senegal."

If I had been drinking water, I would have spit it out! I was so shocked! Senegal doesn't have as few missionaries as Mauritania, but it doesn't have a large missionary population either. It was no coincidence. I called my friend over; and like a giddy little school child, I told him I was going to meet a missionary from Senegal when I returned home. He was so excited that he came back to the States with me to meet him!

In June of that same year, we attended Camp BIMI. Baptist International Missions, Inc. hosts an annual missionary camp at their headquarters in Harrison, Tennessee. The camp consists of mission classes and services led and taught by veteran missionaries. I had already attended my first week at the age of 16 and was looking forward to my second week, especially since I knew where I was going as a missionary. The first service was held in the Lee Roberson Auditorium on a Sunday night. My friend and I sat in the front row, as close as we could get to the action.

We could barely contain our excitement. That evening, the keynote speaker was Ron Bragg, who was at that time the African director. He was also the father of the missionary with whom we had planned to work. Brother Bragg spent 18 years as a missionary in Senegal and was instrumental in starting the work that continues in St. Louis, Senegal, to this day. We wanted desperately to tell him our plans for Senegal, but we stuck to our original decision to let God confirm His leading without human interference.

Brother Bragg opened his Bible and read the text: I Corinthians 16:9, "For a great door and effectual is opened unto me, and there are many adversaries." In his strong Appalachian accent, he announced, "I would like to preach a message tonight entitled 'What it takes to be a missionary in a place like Senegal, West Africa." I'm sure my jaw dropped as he spoke those words. He proceeded to preach on every topic that my friend and I had discussed during the school year. He talked about the need for a pioneer spirit in missions. He spoke on the need to work as a team. He urged us just to do something for God, step out by faith and let God lead. Tears welled up in my eyes, so much so that the room was a blur by the time the service ended.

After his closing prayer, I sat there in an awed silence, overwhelmed at God's precision in confirmation. My friend and I couldn't even look at each other. It was as if God placed His hand on our hearts and said, "You guys have got a good plan. Go for it." We sat speechless for a several minutes as the others around us returned to their rooms.

By the time we regained our composure, Dr. Bragg was making his way out of the building. We caught up to him and told him of our plan to work with his son. We shared with him how we had pulled Mauritania out of a hat and decided to go to Senegal instead. He laughed at our story and wept for joy over what God was doing. He gave us a big bear hug and told us to meet him in his office the next morning. Rising early the next day, we made our way to his office. He contacted his son to tell him of our plan to work with him. His son listened intently as his dad told him about these two guys who wanted to join him in the work in the near future. There was a pause and the voice on the phone replied, "Dad, that's great. We've been praying for a couple of years that God would send us two families to join us in the work."

The Foundation of Every Decision

The first step that every believer must take in the direction toward the fulfillment of the Great Commission is one taken on their knees. The longer I journey forward with the Lord in the work of the ministry, the more I understand how so much of His leading in my life has been the direct result of prayer. I believe that behind every missionary who is called to the mission field is someone on their knees pleading with God to send laborers.

The primary reason we are seeing fewer young people called to the mission field is because fewer parents are pleading with God to call their children into the ministry. Prayer is the driving factor behind the creation of a personnel force for world evangelism. Missions is God's work, and He is seeking those who would join him in this grand endeavor. He has commanded His children to *"pray the Lord of the harvest that he send forth laborers into his harvest."*

I believe the lack of missionaries in the work of God can be attributed to a lack of prayer. It can also be attributed to the emphasis of our pursuits. Rather than urging (or rather, requiring) our children to spend at least a year at Bible college, we encourage them to pursue a "practical career." Some young people feel led into ministry but have been counselled to seek a fallback degree in case the ministry doesn't work out. Jesus said that "no man, having put his hand to the plough, and looking back, is fit for the kingdom of God" (Luke 9:62). We need a new generation of followers of Christ who will recklessly abandon the pursuits of this world and intentionally surrender to the uttermost. We need a generation of men and women who will go with purpose, determined to manifest the name of Christ to every corner of the planet. If you are praying that God would call your child to the ministry, you will be actively encouraging them to pursue seeking the Lord's will.

The triumphant missionary spirit of the New Testament church will be restored to this generation only through prayer and surrender. Ye have not because ye ask not. Fathers and mothers are not pleading with God to send their children to the mission field. Young men and women are no longer pursuing the uttermost with reckless abandon. We need a revival of New Testament missionary spirit. I met a retired pastor in New Brunswick, Canada, who told me that when he was young and had surrendered to God's will to preach, he assumed he was to go where there where no preachers. He set his sights on Algeria until sickness forced him to stay in Canada, where he planted several churches. We need that same spirit today!

Another reason why so few preacher boys consider missions is partly that the church has unintentionally created a false mystique around the concept of being a missionary. Don't get me wrong, I do believe that we should honor those who serve the Lord. Missionaries, evangelists, and pastors make better heroes than the average athlete or actor. But at the same time, we need to remember that missionaries are just ordinary people. The God who calls the missionary is the One who is extraordinary. God delights to use ordinary men and women to do great things: "But God hath chosen the foolish things of the world to confound the wise; and God hath chosen the weak things of the world to confound the things which are mighty" (1 Corinthians 1:27). If you say, "I could never do that!" Good. You are a good candidate for ministry, especially missions. Now all you need is the faith to see God do the improbable through you.

We tend to believe that going to a mission field as a church planter is beyond our ability. You are right if you believe this to be true. Doing God's work is beyond our ability. Our job is not to bring great ability to the altar of God's service. We are called to die to self and simply obey God's command. He will supply the ability to serve. We should determine to go to a field based on the command to go—not on a feeling. Who feels like leaving family and friends and the security and comfort of North America for the frustration of life in a third-world country? Who feels like leaving everything you know for the unknown?

When it comes to knowing God's will, we are better off basing our decisions in life on the Word of God, not on our feelings of ability or adequacy. God will supply all the provision necessary to fulfill His Word and work if we will but obey Him. Paul declared that we are "not sufficient of ourselves to think anything as of ourselves; but our sufficiency is of God" (2 Corinthians 3:5).

I believe that the primary reason God called me to missions is not because of some special ability I possess. My grandmother is the reason I am serving as a missionary. After returning to the States for our first furlough, she shared with me how that as a young girl she surrendered to be a missionary. She met and married my grandfather, who was training to be a pastor in Michigan. After committing her life to serving the Lord as the wife of a pastor, she began praying that the Lord would send one of her children or future grandchildren to the mission field. My call to missions was an answer to that prayer!

Proverbs 16:3 says, "Commit thy works unto the Lord and thy thoughts shall be established." Not until we present our lives a living sacrifice or until we die to self at the altar of surrender through prayer, will we ever begin to understand God's will for our lives. Romans 12 tells us that finding the good, perfect, and acceptable will of God is preceded by the transformation of our minds. We can only be transformed into His image through obedience to the Word of God and surrender in prayer. Pulling a country blindly out of a globe was exciting and set the direction of my life. But reading books such as Praying Hyde and the works of E. M. Bounds set the course of my spiritual life.

We bathe every ministry decision in prayer. We are currently working on a large evangelistic campaign for Senegal, coordinating with both nationals and believers from North America. We are in the beginning planning stage: we pray. Missions is God's idea. It's His work. We can accomplish great things for God only when we are surrendered in prayer to His will and empowered by His Spirit through obedience to His Word.

Finding a Wife

My marriage was an answer to prayer. Certainly, when the Lord gave me my wife, He was answering my prayer for a godly mate. But once Julie and I met, we soon discovered that our marriage itself was also the answer to the specific prayer of her sister. I mentioned earlier that I knew I was going to marry Julie before we had met in person. I know what you might be thinking, but I did not randomly pull her name out of a hat like we did when choosing Senegal!

I met Julie's sister at a Bible camp in Ontario during the summer of 2003. At that time, I was dating another girl, and Julie was engaged to my dorm supervisor! Her family did not feel that the man she was engaged to was the right guy for her. When her sister met me at camp, where her husband was the keynote speaker, she felt that Julie and I would make a great pair. She began praying, unbeknownst to us both, that the Lord would put us together. For that to happen, we both had to part ways with our current interests.

By Christmas of the same year, I was no longer dating; and through an email, Julie's fiancé broke off their engagement on the day before Christmas Eve. Even while Julie was still heartbroken, her sister called her and recommended that she consider dating me. Julie was neither interested in nor impressed with the suggestion.

Now that we were both available, there remained one more obstacle. We had never met. Her brother and I were roommates, I knew her two sisters, but Julie and I had not met. She had graduated the year before I went to college and was teaching in a Christian school an hour north of Toronto. She knew me only by reputation through her brother, and I knew her only as the girl my dorm supervisor was going to marry but decided not to. Also, I knew she made really good brownies which I would steal from her brother's care packages that she would send.

About six weeks after I returned to college from winter break, a desire, seemingly springing up from nowhere, took root in my mind. The thought basically said, "Why don't you go for Julie? Pursue her!" I didn't know what to think. I had never met Julie. Was this the Lord speaking or the brownies she had made that I had stolen from her brother? I decided that I would treat this desire the same way I treated our plan to go to Senegal. If God was behind this, He would reveal it in His time. The thought grew stronger in my mind and the desire to meet her grew more intense. In the midst of my wrestling with the idea of pursuing a girl I had never met, I was asked to film a promotional video for a church in St. Thomas, Ontario.

I made my way down to the church, completely unaware of what I was about to walk into. Upon arriving, I was greeted by the assistant pastor. He just so happened to have been the keynote speaker at the Bible camp I had attended the year prior and was the husband of Julie's sister. The same sister who has been praying for the past eight months that Julie and I would get together. The sister who had already mentioned her prayer to Julie, but not to me. Had I known what she was praying, I probably would have responded differently to her husband's question about my dating life.

When he asked me if I was seeing anyone, I had the bright idea—which actually popped right out of my mouth—of suggesting that I marry Julie. My reasoning was that since her brother, my good friend and roommate, was also getting married that summer, and since Julie had planned to get married as well (albeit she was not without a groom), I should marry her so that her brother and I could live off campus and hang out. I'm not sure why I said this except that I was trying to get a feel for what God was doing in my heart. I did not expect his response.

He had a stunned look on his face as he called over his wife. "Tell my wife what you just said, Josh." I started sweating and was probably flushed as I sheepishly repeated what I had said. I had barely finished the final sentence before she blurted out, "Would you? Would you marry her? I've been praying for this for the past year and I know that God answers my prayers!"

I didn't know what to say. All I could think of was *what if Julie finds out that some creep she's never met is talking about marrying her* followed by *why are they so eager to marry her off?* As I drove home that evening, I knew in my mind that God was at work. The desire was on my heart, and her sister had been praying for it: two major indications that God is at work. Julie was the girl I was going to marry.

I've got to meet her, I thought to myself.

Exactly one week later I was asked to choose two guys and travel to North Bay, Ontario, to preach in a small church where the pastor had recently resigned. I chose two roommates and made the four-hour trip north. On the way, we passed the city where Julie was residing. I tried thinking of an excuse to justify stopping in and meeting her. Then I realized that the pianist who was with me was from the same city. I had a reason to visit the city, but still had no reason to visit Julie. Then I realized that the other preacher boy that I had chosen was dating a girl who was sitting out a semester and living with her parents in this city. Julie rented their basement apartment!

Now I had a good reason to stop at the very house where Julie lived. After the Sunday evening service, on our way back to the college, I asked the guys if they wanted to make a pit stop in Barrie (the city where Julie lived). They were more than happy to do so. I'll never forget seeing Julie in person for the first time. She came into the upstairs kitchen where we were enjoying some desserts. I had a half-eaten muffin in my hand when she rounded the corner. It was as if the world stopped turning. I was speechless.

After regaining my words, we chatted for a bit. I assumed that she was oblivious as to my intentions for being there. I was really nervous, and I'm sure it showed. We said our goodbyes and headed back to the college. I kept thinking to myself, this is definitely the girl I'm going to marry. I couldn't wait to see her again.

FaithWay Baptist College of Canada hosted an annual student convention. Christian schools from across Ontario came to compete in fine arts and sporting events. Julie accompanied her junior high class. This was my opportunity to speak with her about my intentions. The final night of the convention, I worked up the nerve to ask her for her number.

The next time we spoke at length, she told me her side of the story about the first time we met. She shared how that minutes before my unannounced arrival in Barrie, her sister had called her. The entire conversation concerned what I had said the week prior when I mentioned being interested in marrying her. Julie was confused as to how someone could be interested in her when we had never met. Her sister assured her it was an answer to prayer. In the middle of the conversation, she was interrupted by visitors at the door. She said goodbye to her sister, made her way upstairs, and, to her surprise, there I was standing in her kitchen, eating a muffin!

That night she told the Lord that if it was His will, she would go wherever He was leading. Even before we began officially dating, I showed her the video from my survey trip to Senegal and told her of my plans to work there. She replied, "I never thought I'd be a missionary, but it is very clear that God has put us together."

Prayer is the most important aspect and the most vital work of missions. The Bible is our instruction manual, the Holy Spirit is our Guide, and prayer is the means of communicating and receiving that guidance. Prayer is how we get more missionaries to the mission field. Prayer is how we find God's will. Prayer is how God works in and through us. The depth of the incredible spiritual power of the first century church was in direct correlation to their prayer lives.

The surest way to discover God's will for your life is to pray the Bible. Claim the promises of Scripture. Ask for wisdom, seek His face and knock at the door of God's grace until it opens wide to you. Most of the time, living and working in a foreign culture, I have no idea what to do or how to respond to certain circumstances. God promises abundant wisdom if we will simply ask by faith. The most intense times of God forming me during my college years was alone, on my knees at the bottom of a stairwell with a Bible opened in front of me. If you don't have a prayer life and don't know where

71

to begin, I suggest getting on your knees and reading the Scripture out loud. You will develop a prayer life sooner than you could imagine.

Going to Senegal, Was an Answer to an Unbeliever's Prayer!

The testimony of a man in our church in Senegal again confirmed the importance of prayer. The first man we led to the Lord was originally from a neighboring country but was residing in Senegal. He had been sent by his family to study Islam in the highly respected Quranic schools of our city. His uncle was one of the most powerful and influential imams in his home country. His entire family is Muslim. I taught him the Bible for one year before he was ready to personally receive Christ. He would travel back to his home village during the harvest and return to our city to continue studying the Bible for the remainder of the year. We continued to disciple him for several years.

He was hesitant to reveal his new faith to his family for fear of his uncle. At the time, I did not realize how serious a threat this family member was. During one of his visits home, his uncle found his notebook with Bible verses written inside. While the young man did not reveal his faith in Christ, he was still beaten and hospitalized simply for having neglected the memorization of the Quran and instead studying the Bible. His uncle confiscated his identity card, essentially imprisoning him in his home. After being released from the hospital, he was locked in a room for a couple of weeks. One evening he was able to escape when someone forgot to lock the door.

He returned to our city and shared the details of what had happened. His courage was inspiring. A visitor we were hosting on a mission trip asked him what sparked his interest in Jesus. He told us that someone had come to his village when he was younger and showed the Jesus film. He was drawn to the teaching and compassion of Jesus. He read how that Jesus taught His followers to love and pray for their enemies. Islam does not teach this. He asked God to send him a Christian who could teach him the truth of the Bible. When he met me, he knew in his heart that what we were teaching was true, that we practiced what we taught, and that God had answered his prayer.

If the story ended there, we can say it is truly an incredible story. But there was more to the story. Before he returned to his room that night, I asked him when it was that he first prayed for God to send him a Christian teacher. He thought for a minute and replied, "I believe it was in 2002." I smiled, overjoyed with amazement. The year 2002 was also the same year that we randomly choose to work in Senegal. Blindly choosing a pioneer country out of a globe was not only an answer to our prayer, but it was also a direct answer to the prayer of a seeker in Senegal! There are no coincidences in the work of God. The Bible is true when it promises that God will direct our steps.

But in order for God to direct future steps in your ministry, you sometimes have to be willing to take the next step by faith.

PART TWO: The Next Step

The Difference Between Knowing God's Will

and Doing It

You have felt God's call and responded to it. Although not sure where you would end up, you began Bible school with confidence that God would guide your path. You were stretched and molded during your school years. You endured unto the end and have finally received the crowning reward of your achievement, a Bible college diploma.

If you are like many Bible college students, you probably find yourself staring down at your diploma saying to yourself, "Now what? Where do I go? What is the next step?" Whether you have reached this point in your life, are still working toward it or your college years are far behind you, figuring out where God wants you is never easy. It's okay to not be sure of exactly where God wants you to serve. What God might want you to do right now is to take the next step by faith. You might reply, "But I am not sure if this is the right step to take." That's alright. The step of faith is the step that God will bless. The difference between knowing God's will and doing it is whether or not you take the next step right in front of you.

Of course, the next step is not always obvious and that, too, is okay. Kevin DeYoung writes, "God is not a Magic 8-Ball we shake up and peer into whenever we have a decision to make. He is a good God who gives us brains, shows us the way of obedience, and invites us to take risks for him."

It's About the What of the Where Not the Where of the What

Young people going into the ministry are often consumed with trying to discover where God wants them to serve. The *where* of your calling is not as important right now as it is for you to grasp the *what* of your calling. We need a revolution of going back to the Bible concerning what it means to be called to preach. A call to preach is first and foremost a call to be separated unto God and unto His gospel (Romans 1:1; Galatians 1:15).

Remember, being separated unto the gospel implies that we are commanded to be going where the gospel is not known. Jesus gave the marching orders to the church: "Go ye into all the world and preach the gospel to every creature." Paul writes in Romans 10, explaining that to fulfill this commission, the church must send preachers to those who have never heard. "How then shall they call on him in whom they have not believed? and how shall they believe in him of whom they have not heard? and how shall they hear without a preacher? And how shall they preach, except they be sent? as it is written, How beautiful are the feet of them that preach the gospel of peace, and bring glad tidings of good things" (Romans 10:14-15).

The God-called preacher must be ready to go to the uttermost at a moment's notice. Philip was called to a desert place while he was preaching in a dynamic and fruitful revival campaign in Samaria. The Bible says in Acts 8:27 that Philip, without hesitation, "arose and went." Philip knew what he was called to do: preach. Where he preached was a matter of the leading of God. God may ask you to stay in your home culture or He may ask you to leave everything and go to a desert place. If you are called of God to gospel ministry, you have one primary objective, to preach Christ. Learn to develop the gifts that God has given you for the ministry. Learn to be *what* God wants you to be. Many ask God to show them *where* they could go to be most effective. Ask God to help you learn to become effective where you are.

The Holy Spirit separates and calls believers who are actively serving in the local church. He reveals His calling to those who have been saved and who are surrendered. If you have sensed God's call, especially His call to preach, you have an obligation to consider the Biblical teaching that you have been separated to go. You must understand what it means to be separated unto the gospel. The directive of your calling is the Great Commission; its fulfillment is your objective; and God's glory is the result.

Being a witness for Christ is all about the glory of God. Christianity is not about what God can do for us. Grace is not primarily about the benefits that we can get out of salvation. We did not receive the Holy Spirit and His power for our own benefit alone. Jesus told His disciples that they would receive power, after that the Holy Ghost was come upon them. He didn't tell them that they would then have the power to heal the sick, speak in other tongues, and raise the dead. Some of these signs followed the day of Pentecost, but they were not the primary purpose of the Spirit indwelling.

The coming of the Spirit of God was to empower believers to be witnesses of Christ unto the uttermost. We are stewards of the gospel of God, commanded to be fruitful and to multiply and to fill the earth with the knowledge of the saving grace of Jesus Christ. We are commanded to preach to every creature and make disciples in every nation. Because the individual believer is the "temple of the Holy Ghost which is in you" (I Corinthians 6:19), mission is no longer centralized around a physical temple as it was for the nation of Israel. God's plan of operation is to send the church to every nation, to go to the uttermost, where Christ is not named. True Christianity and the fulfillment of the Great Commission in the power of the Spirit is all about the glory of God.

For the Apostle Paul, the imperative of the command was clear. He shares his mission statement and ministry philosophy in Romans 15:20: "Yea, so have I strived to preach the gospel, not where Christ was named, lest I should build upon another man's foundation." If more young men and women called to ministry were to embrace this same biblical mindset we would see more laborers advancing toward the unreached peoples of the world.

Is the objective of pioneering the gospel where Christ is not named only for a unique few among the many who are called into ministry? I don't believe so. Paul based this

79

mission statement not on a unique calling, a fuzzy feeling, or even on the need of the lost. His directive was based on the clear

The difference between knowing God's will and doing it is whether you take the next step right in front of you.

command of Scripture. He supports this mission statement with a quotation from the Old Testament. Verse 21 says, "But as it is written, To whom he was not spoken of, they shall see: and they that have not heard shall understand."

I'm sure most of Paul's contemporaries felt that he could be greatly used in the city of Rome. He himself had even expressed his desire to preach to them the gospel in chapter one of Romans. But he clearly states the reason he had not yet visited the established church in that city. Paul had a passion for preaching the gospel, particularly preaching where Christ was not known. He continues in Romans 15:22, "For which cause also I have been much hindered from coming to you." What hindered Paul from visiting and serving in a city where there was already an established church? What was the cause that kept him from what others would assume to be a perfect fit for his gifting and ministry? His education and abilities, after all, seemed to suggest he was better suited to be used in Rome rather than some obscure city that consisted of only a handful of believers.

What kept Paul from visiting Rome was his calling to fulfill the Great Commission. Until his region (Paul was in Corinth when he wrote the book of Romans) had adequate access to the gospel, he wasn't going anywhere, no matter how tempting the offer of bigger and better things might have appeared. Not until he fulfilled his work and had "no more place in these parts" (Romans 15:23) did he feel he could visit the church at Rome. Even then, he was only passing through

A Biblical call to preach is to consider first where the gospel is not yet preached and to move forward to go there.

on his way to evangelize the unreached region of Spain. Romans 15:24 states, "Whensoever I take my journey into Spain, I will come to you: for I trust to see you in my journey, and to be brought on my way thitherward by you, if first I be somewhat filled with your company." He had plans to visit the church at Rome only so as to allow them to help him pioneer the gospel to Spain. God's glory reaching the uttermost was his only ambition. The anthem of the Great Commission is recorded in Psalm 72:19 and was written on Paul's heart: "Let the whole earth be filled with his glory! Amen, and Amen."

At the core of Paul's understanding of what it meant to be called and to be separated unto the gospel was a passion to preach where people had never heard the truth of Christ. I believe that if we start with the *what* of the calling (the command to go to the uttermost), the *where* of our service will become self-evident. I challenge you to tell the Lord that you will take a step of faith toward the unreached people groups of the world. This step of obedience to the Great Commission is the fulfillment of your calling unto the gospel service. If you take the first step by faith, God will guide your next step. You can't even begin to imagine what God has in store for you when you are willing to jump out of the boat by faith.

Don't Assume You're Meant to Stay, Assume You're Called to Go

It is possible that we in North America have created a false assumption that a call to preach is an automatic call to the pastorate in your home country. We've convinced ourselves that becoming a foreign missionary is a unique calling to a qualified few. I asked one young man if he had considered becoming a missionary. "I'm called to preach, not to be a missionary" was his reply.

The term missionary is not found in the Bible. The term may help missionaries define what their occupation is, but I believe it has unintentionally put a chasm between the call to preach and the command to go. Going, and especially going in the direction of the uttermost, is the main directive to the calling to ministry. A Biblical call to preach is to consider first where the gospel is not yet preached and to move forward to go there. It is time that young men rise up like the Apostle Paul and declare "I will strive to preach the gospel, not where Christ is named" (Romans 15:20).

A young man once asked me how he can know if God wants him to serve as a missionary in an unreached place or to serve as a pastor in America. Besides sharing the principles of Paul's mission philosophy and the command to go from Jesus Himself, I shared my own heart experience. At some point in seeking God's will for my life as a preacher, I had to ask myself this question: Do I want to spend my life's work and ministry sharing the gospel with people who have abundant access to the truth? Where there is a church on every corner; where both on the radio and television we can generally find a clear gospel presentation? Or, do I have a burning passion to take the gospel to a people who have never heard the gospel clearly presented? Do I yearn to pioneer the gospel to a people who, if I were not there, may never have an opportunity to hear the truth in their lifetime?

I believe that if we have a revolution back to the Bible concerning God's call, there will be a revival in the missionary labor force. If we return to the Scriptures as the source for our decision making in ministry, we will find the evangelization of the world within our reach in our generation. We are called to go to the nations for the glory of God. We are called to go make disciples by the command of Christ. We are called to go into all the world for love's sake. Jesus commanded us to "Go therefore and make disciples of all nations" (Matthew 28:19). The imperative verb in verse 19 is "make disciples," not "go." In other words, based upon the finished work of Christ and His authority, we are commanded to make disciples; the "going" is assumed in the command. You cannot make disciples of all nations (*ethnos*) unless you are going to the nations. The church is not fulfilling her calling to make disciples unless she is actively sending preachers to the unreached peoples of the world.

We need an awakening to the Biblical mission of evangelizing the nations. The mission to make the truth known. The mission to live righteous and holy lives. We have been given a mission to make Christ known to all people groups. It *is* the will of God. "Awake to righteousness, and sin not," Paul declares. "For some have not the knowledge of the gospel: I speak this to your shame" (1 Corinthians 15:34).

Are we ashamed that God's glory is being trampled and mocked in modern western nations? Are we ashamed that 55,000 people die every day who have had no access to the gospel? Are we ashamed that the truth of Christ is blasphemed through the false teachings of many of the world's major religions? Are we ashamed that Christ is misrepresented in most nations; or are we ashamed that He is not represented at all in others?

The term *10/40 Window* was coined almost three decades ago to bring awareness to the over 5 billion people residing within this geographical location. After three decades of awareness still 68% of the people living in the 10/40 Window are considered unreached. We are living in a time of unparalleled prosperity and limitless opportunities whereby we have the means share the gospel in these nations. Why are so few willing to go?

I'll Go...Just Not Yet

Maybe you have reasoned with yourself and it sounded something like this: "I am not ashamed of the gospel of God. I am ready to preach the gospel where Christ is not named. But I just graduated from college. I would like to get some practical experience first."

I've heard this reasoning from several students who have shared with me their desire to go into mission work.

Leaving everything you know and all that is familiar to you and moving to a distant land is an intimidating thought. Not everyone is ready for deputation and the mission field straight out of college. Practical training is important and essential. Waiting of God's timing is absolutely necessary.

On the other hand, I have seen far too many young men, having expressed a desire to serve in missions, get comfortable in a secure position in a big church somewhere in North America. They soon get bogged down with debt and even use the excuse of starting a family to delay their launching out into the deep. One excuse leads to another and before they know it, the desire to go to the foreign field fades into a distant memory that only existed in an impractical, romantic, youthful mind.

One pastor suggested to me that if a young man or woman doesn't have the gumption to go and ends up staying home, they were probably never called to go in the first place. I disagree with this sentiment. As we have already considered, Jesus commanded us to go into all the world and preach the gospel to every creature. If someone expresses a desire in his youth to go abroad as a missionary, let's not assume it's only a temporary fanciful, romantic dream of youthful wanderlust. The majority of missionaries I know felt called into world evangelism in their youth.

The problem is not God's calling. What is holding back most young people from launching out into the uttermost is a lack of personal surrender—not surrender to God but surrender to the unknown. Some fit the John Mark personality and simply may not be ready to launch out into a life of the unknown. Not everyone has the personality of a Paul or a Peter.

On the other hand, there are those who seem the most qualified for the task of world evangelism and yet return home to their sending country after only one or two terms of service. Mission work is exciting, but if you are not mentally prepared for the challenges, you risk becoming another statistic of the high missionary turn-over rate. Many pastors and mission board leaders will agree that a discouraging and sometimes frustrating aspect of supporting and sending missionaries is what can simply be termed as the missionary attrition rate.

For one reason or another, missionaries leave the mission field and return to their country of origin. One survey revealed that over a 10-year period, most mission agencies will retain only 50% of their missionaries; and nearly 60% of those leaving, resign for potentially preventable reasons[1]. In

---

[1] Van Meter, Jim (2003, December) US Report of Findings on Missionary Retention. Retrieved from http://www.worldevangelicals.org

other words, if a mission agency has 100 missionaries, within 10 years 50 missionaries will resign, 30 of whom could potentially have been prevented from leaving—and the problem is not getting better.

I believe that there are three primary types of missionary candidates: The Paul/Barnabas type, the John Mark type, and the Timothy type. We would do well to recognize which personality type we fit into before we consider launching out into the unknown. We need all three types of missionaries on the foreign field.

As we break down these categories of missionary candidates, we will discover that it is usually the Paul/Barnabas type who are ready and willing to go at a moment's notice. The John Mark type are willing to go in spirit, but they may not be prepared for the physical and mental challenges and therefore do not remain long on the field. They need extended preparation.

Then there is the Timothy type. There are not many under this category of personality who go to the mission field. They are generally so reserved and practical that they rarely step out into the unknown. But it is men and women like Timothy who are the backbone of effective ministries. When the Timothy type does surrender to go, he is in it for the long haul.

The one who fits the Paul/Barnabas type of missionary candidate tends to have what we call the 'type A' personality. Both Paul and Barnabas were natural, self-disciplined, and self-motivated leaders. Paul had tendencies of being more aggressive and ambitious in his vision and execution of mission. He described his personal discipline habits in I Corinthians 9:27 when he penned, "But I keep under my body, and bring it into subjection: lest that by any means, when I have preached to others, I myself should be a castaway."

Paul was ambitious. When he met Christ, his personal ambition turned into an unrelenting passion to fulfill the Great Commission. He had once exerted the utmost fervor into hunting down and killing the followers of Jesus the Nazarene. He believed he was defending the name of God and would seek to honor what he thought was right no matter who stood in his way. With that same feverish passion, he would turn to hunting down and winning to Christ those who had never heard the gospel. In the case of his dealings with John Mark, Paul was moving forward for this cause no matter who stood in his way, even if it meant parting ways with his own mentor, Barnabas.

Barnabas was also a natural leader, having ambition and passion to reach the world. But he was more apt to emphasize compassion, patience, and encouragement in his leadership than was Paul. Second chances were part of his second nature. He saw the potential of what could be. Paul only saw what should be. Paul was prone to leave you behind in the dust if you did not meet his standard of what he thought you should be. Barnabas was there to pick you up when you fell.

Don't think I am maligning the Paul type. We need men like Paul in the ministry. Paul *was* compassionate, but to him, there was no time to waste with quitters. Barnabas did not see a quitter in John Mark. He saw a young man who was not yet prepared for the life of the unknown. John simply needed more time to prepare and someone to encourage him to not give up.

Both types of men are necessary in the ministry. These are the men who have a clear calling of God in their lives. They have vision. They have purpose. They know their calling and need no man to tell them the direction they should take. At times it seemed that Paul would even get ahead of the Spirit's leadership (Acts 16)!

Not everyone called to missionary work is a Paul or Barnabas. We need more Paul's, and we definitely need more men like Barnabas. There are, however, other types of personalities that God uses. I think it would be safe to say that the majority of men called to preach fit either the John Mark and Timothy type rather than the Paul/Barnabas type. The John Mark type are those who are called to serve in ministry and are willing to go to the uttermost, but they might not be mentally or physically ready for the challenge of mission work in the unknown.

We first hear of John Mark in Luke's record of the Acts of the Apostles in the twelfth chapter. His home was more than likely a primary meeting place for the church in Jerusalem. As persecution grew and they were expelled from the Temple, believers would meet in homes for worship and study. John Mark was no stranger to the risks of being associated with Christ. He saw firsthand the persecution of the fledgling church in Jerusalem. He willingly volunteered to join his uncle Barnabas and Paul on their first missionary journey (Acts 13:5).

We are not sure why John Mark left the missionary team shortly after launching out from Antioch. One might conclude that he was a coward, and that is why he parted ways with Paul and Barnabas in Acts 13:13. Paul seemed to have thought so. In Acts 15:37-38, the Bible says, "And Barnabas determined to take with them John, whose surname was Mark. But Paul thought not good to take him with them, who departed from them from Pamphylia, and went not with them to the work." Was Paul right to refuse to give John Mark a second chance? Was John Mark a coward? Was he afraid of the risks?

In Mark 14:51-52, John Mark records the following incident: "And there followed him a certain young man, having a linen cloth cast about his naked body; and the young men laid hold on him: And he left the linen cloth, and fled from them naked." It appears that the young man who fled naked from those who came to arrest Christ was John Mark himself. Sure, he fled like a coward. But so did all the other disciples. Yet likewise, just as the disciples of Christ, he received a new-found courage on the day of Pentecost with the arrival of indwelling Spirit.

He had matured exponentially by the time he volunteered to join Barnabas and Paul. I believe John Mark did not leave the mission team primarily because of the risks. I don't believe he was a coward. I believe he left because he was not prepared spiritually and mentally to leave the safety net of a support system. After facing the reality of missionary life, John Mark decided he was not ready and returned, not to

Antioch, but home to Jerusalem. What was in Jerusalem? His mother. His support system. His comfort zone. It is one thing to be persecuted for your faith when you have family and friends to back you up. It is quite another when you are alone. John was not ready for the harsh realities of the missionary life in the unknown. Roland Allen makes a similar suggestion in his book *Missionary Methods.*

> The most natural explanation of the return of John Mark from Perga is that he turned back because he saw that after the crisis at Paphos St. Paul was become the real leader of the mission in the place of his own cousin, Barnabas, and was prepared both to preach outside the synagogue to Gentiles with greater freedom than he had anticipated, and to admit Gentiles into fellowship on terms which he was hardly proposing to accept. He saw too that St. Paul was proposing to penetrate into regions more remote, perhaps more dangerous, than he had expected. In other words, there was at Perga a real change both in the direction and in the character of the mission.[2]

_____

[2] Allen, Roland *MIssionary Methods, St. Paul's or Ours? Wm. B. Eerdmans Publishing Co.1962, Pg. 32*

While I do not necessarily agree with his statement that John Mark was not ready to accept Gentiles into fellowship, I do believe that the prospect of penetrating remote regions with the gospel was more than he was ready to handle. He was not fearful of opposition as much as he was fearful of facing the unknown. He was no coward. He simply was not ready to face the devil square in the eyes in the devil's own backward without a stronger support system about him. John was willing to sacrifice his life for Christ. He knew the risk and gladly surrendered to go. He saw God deliver Peter from prison. He accompanied Barnabas on his mission to Antioch. He was willing to go and to serve at any cost. But willingness is not the same as readiness. The reality of working with an unknown language in an unknown culture, living among people whose way of life and thinking is unknown to the missionary can be overwhelming and stressful.

John Mark quickly found himself launched deep into the heart of the enemy's territory. He quickly realized that when the going got tough, they had no one to turn to for support and encouragement but themselves and the Lord. The call to the uttermost is a call to loneliness. Unlike David at Ziklag, John Mark had not yet learned to encourage himself in the Lord. There is a level of spiritual maturity required for mission work that can be measured only when you are actually tested on the field. John's abandoning the team did not mean that he was not qualified or not called to go to the uttermost. It simply means he was not ready.

I recently spoke with a BIMI missionary who has served 40 years in Niger. The Lord has greatly used this couple to spread the gospel through a gospel radio program that broadcasts throughout Niger, parts of Libya, as well as Nigeria. He recently received news that 20 men in a village received Christ after listening to the broadcast. He shared with me that many westerners are not interested in working in places like Niger, for many reasons. One reason is the isolation they would face. He told me of a couple who came, passionate to share the gospel, but not ready live a life cut off from a support system. After 15 months on the field, they packed up and returned home.

Americans are moving more and more *away* from the type of lifestyle required to live in a place like rural Niger. The shock on their system is just too much for them. Yet I know that God can raise up another Charles Studd ("Give me a rescue shop within a yard of hell!"), or another Saul ("…necessity is laid upon me; yea, woe is unto me, if I preach not the gospel!"). And should God call anyone, that is enough! He is the LORD of the Harvest!

Willingness is Not the Same as Readiness

I believe that practical, on-the-field training is essential to preparing a missionary candidate for longevity on the mission field. Extended internship programs, much like BIMI's The Next Step Internship (which we will introduce later in the book), are designed to help the John Mark type of missionary candidate better prepare for the reality of the loneliness of reaching the uttermost. Sometimes only reality can prepare us for effective ministry. But it is important that the missionary candidate not face the initial reality alone. Team work is essential, not only in execution of mission but in preparation for effective long-term mission service.

The country of Jordan has a small but effective military. The king of Jordan recently gave an interview to *60 Minutes* in which he attributed part of their success to the fact that they use live ammunition in every training situation! Intensive, practical, and reality-based training is key to long-term effectiveness.

The Timothy Type: Timid but Willing

The Apostle Paul often recruited young men to labor alongside with him. Once he found a candidate, he would ask him to join him on the field immediately. Timothy was one such candidate who was ready for the reality of the unknown. There are a few principles we find in Scripture that helped form Timothy into a young man ready to launch out into the preparation stage of mission work. In Acts 16, Paul returned to Lystra to strengthen the brethren. On this return trip, his path crossed with an outstanding young man who would prove to be an invaluable partner in Paul's future ministry.

> Then came he to Derbe and Lystra: and, behold, a certain disciple was there named Timotheus, the son of a certain woman…Which was well reported of by the brethren that were at Lystra…Him would Paul have to go forth. (Acts 16:1-3)

Luke refers to Timothy as a certain man who was the son of a certain woman. In other words, this was an everyday disciple in an everyday town being raised by an everyday woman. There is no qualification in Timothy that stood out in the mind of Luke which would attract the attention of the Apostle Paul. In fact, Timothy appears to have been a bit timorous. He was known for his faithful steadfastness, not temerarious passion and ambition. God simply requires faithfulness of His stewards, a character trait manifest in

> *No man is ready for the mission field who is not first faithful in his local church.*

Timothy that would eventually lead him to become Paul's right-hand man.

Paul recognized that Timothy would make a valuable addition to their mission team. Sometimes God uses other people to help us recognize our potential for serving God: "Him would Paul have to go forth" (Acts 16:3). Leaders need to be able to recognize these qualities in potential recruits. Young men and women surrendered to the will of God need to be sensitive when God uses others in their lives to help direct their paths.

What qualified Timothy for this task? First of all, he had a healthy relationship with his local church. No man is ready for the mission field who is not first faithful in his local church. At this point, it bears remarking that Timothy may not have yet sensed his calling to the foreign field, but he was ready nonetheless.

"a certain disciple was there...well reported of by the brethren."

No man or woman can be a true disciple of Christ without having a strong attachment to and loyalty for their local church. The church in Lystra knew Timothy. This young man loved God, was faithful to church, and served God fervently. Just as the Apostle Paul, Timothy was called to go while actively involved in his local church. God does not call men and women who are on the inactive roster. He simply moves active servants from one arena to another as He sees fit. Thomas Hale writes, "God's call doesn't register in a vacuum; only a person who is committed to doing God's will can receive a call."[3]

Timothy also had a testimony of fidelity among the brethren. Luke records in Acts 16:2 that Timothy was, "Well reported of by the brethren that were at Lystra and Iconium." Timothy's testimony for God was well known. Here's a young man who many Bible teachers believe had an unbelieving father. Yet the brethren, the men in his local church, would have been proud to have called him their son. He had a blameless testimony in his community. There was no hesitation among the church leadership to recommend this young man to full-time ministry. There was no question as to his character and readiness.

Lastly, Timothy was used because he had a willing spirit to serve at any cost, in any capacity and in any country. Acts 16:3 says, "(H)im would Paul have to go forth with him; and took and circumcised him because of the Jews...." A true

[3] Thomas Hale, *On Being a Missionary* (Pasadena, CA: William Carey Library, 1995), 18

disciple is willing not only to count the cost but is willing to pay the price of following Christ. Are you willing to serve no matter the cost?

At Any Cost

Timothy was literally willing to offer his body a living sacrifice for God! A missionary must be willing to become all things to all men. If Timothy was going to have an effective ministry among the dispersed Jews, he would have to be circumcised. Liberty in Christ does not mean we are to be insensitive to the conscience of others. To serve Christ in the uttermost, we must be ready and willing to adapt to the cultural expectations of the people we are attempting to reach. If we are to be effective for Christ we must be willing to serve at any cost.

When we moved to Senegal I began to wear the long robes that are popular in many African nations. I was given a piece of beautiful blue material as a Christmas gift. I decided to have my tailor make the best robe he could design. I asked him to make the embroidery extra fancy and even to include cuffs on the sleeves for my cufflinks. The first time I wore it in public, I received all kinds of attention from the Senegalese. They loved it!

The candidate qualified for the mission field is first surrendered to serve at any cost.

Everyone complimented me on my robe, including strangers I didn't even know. They loved seeing this white guy wearing traditional African attire. I loved adapting to the cultural expectations of the people I was serving.

Then I made the mistake of wearing it to my home church on our first furlough. I thought I would receive the same praise and attention I had received in Senegal. I thought everyone would admire their missionary who must surely be the next Hudson Taylor, dressing as the people that he might more effectively reach them! I confidently walked into the church foyer only to hear a sarcastic remark from one of our deacons, "Josh, since when did you start wearing dresses?" I protested, "It's not a dress!" Another wise-guy remarked, "It must be nice being a missionary. I wish I could wear my pajamas to church!"

While being made fun of or mocked by people in your church doesn't qualify as persecution, we must all be willing to adapt to the culture of the people whom we are reaching. We must count the cost before launching out. Timothy knew well the price one might suffer when surrendering to the unknown. He had seen Paul beaten and left for dead a few years prior! Read Acts 14. In Paul's initial visit to this city he was not warmly received. Paul went back to the city where he had been beaten and left for dead and asked young Timothy to join his missionary team. I can imagine the conversation with Timothy's mother went something like this:

"Mom, the Apostle Paul has asked me to join his missionary team!"

"Really, the Apostle Paul?"

"Yes! Isn't that exciting!"

"The Apostle Paul? The same Apostle Paul who was beaten and stoned and left for dead the last time he visited? That Apostle Paul?"

"Yes mom, that Apostle Paul."

"Are you sure, Timothy? Are you sure that you want to go?"

At this point, Tim's grandmother might have chimed in: "Let him go Eunice. I've been praying that God would call him to be a missionary. And my prayers get answered!"

Who would have blamed Timothy's mother for having reservations—or any mother whose child announces his desire to move to a foreign land to preach the gospel. A missionary's safety is constantly on the minds of family back home. Despite the reservations, God had a plan for Timothy. The Apostle Paul saw in this young man what Timothy himself could not as yet see: a man of God with specific gifts that would be a great blessing to the mission work.

Timothy was willing to serve anyone and everyone. He was ready to adapt his personal preferences to reach a particular people group. He was willing to lay down his life, his rights, his liberty for the sake of the gospel. The candidate qualified for the mission field is first surrendered to serve at any cost.

In Any Capacity

We are not told of Timothy's role or position at the church in Lystra. He appears to have been involved in some sort of itinerant preaching or teaching ministry in the surrounding local churches. He was well reported of by the brethren in Lystra and Iconium. Joining Paul's team may have meant he took a lesser role in a larger world-wide ministry. God had big plans for Timothy. In the work of the Lord, great things come only to those who serve. Only the humble advance in the work of the Lord. Besides faithfulness, humility to serve in any capacity is the most important characteristic required for usability. We must be willing to serve in any way possible.

While we were on deputation, my grandparents church went through a split. I was asked several times if I would consider pastoring the group of believers who had broken off (for good reason) to form a new church. I was flattered. I do not deny there was an appeal to the thought of pastoring a sizable group of faithful, mature believers.

I was once offered a media job at one of the largest Independent Baptist Churches in America. I am not sharing this because I think that I'm something special. I share this only because we can easily tell ourselves that we could be more effective in a larger ministry in America than we could be on the far side of the desert in some desolate region of the planet. Timothy could have reasoned within himself that staying in his home city made more sense. It was safe. He had a secure position and a sure future. His family was there. He was part of something big. God was working. They needed him.

For Timothy, ministry wasn't about bright lights, a secure paycheck and a safe environment to raise a family. Ministry was surrender to Christ and His command. He was willing to surrender to the unknown of ministry to the uttermost parts of the earth. He was willing to serve in whatever capacity the Lord saw fit, great or small. This qualification and this alone makes you a prime candidate for gospel service, whether at home or abroad: a humble, willing spirit.

In Any Country

Jesus has called us to make disciples of every nation. A true disciple is willing not only to serve in any capacity but to serve in any country.

You might say, "I don't believe God has called me to the uttermost; He has called me to reach my Jerusalem." The problem with that kind of thinking is that Jerusalem in Acts 1:8 simply represents the literal city of Jerusalem. I am not sure why we refer to our home country as our Jerusalem. Most of the Apostles were not originally from Jerusalem, so even Jerusalem was not 'their Jerusalem.'

Jerusalem was the center of religious and civil life for the Jew. Not for the Church. The point Jesus was making is that we have been given a responsibility to make sure that the gospel is available to every nation and ethnicity (*ethnos* in Greek) on earth. The uttermost is not necessarily referring to a specific geographical location. As mentioned earlier, Acts 1:8 is telling us that we, the church, must take the gospel to where the gospel is not. We are commanded to be witnesses, starting where we are.

Today, it is currently illegal to "proselytize" Jews in Israel. Jerusalem, where the gospel first sounded forth, has now become a part of the unreached uttermost! If your hometown has few or no gospel preaching local churches, then that may very well be a part of the uttermost. The uttermost is where the gospel is not easily accessible. The uttermost is where there are few or no preachers and indigenous churches, where Christ is not known.

Timothy could have remained in his hometown and would probably have built a great ministry. However, there were already several local churches in his hometown and the surrounding cities. A deep yearning in the heart of Timothy was calling him to step out by faith in obedience to the Great Commission and pursue the uttermost. Given Timothy's personality, I don't believe it was a sense of adventure or romanticism that put a yearning in his heart to take the gospel to the ends of the earth. Timothy seems to have been more practical, not basing his decisions on a whim of emotion or passion. He thought things through. He knew the command of Christ and understood his calling to preach the gospel to every creature.

There are two responses to seeing or hearing about the struggles, adventures, and persecutions that entail the life of a missionary. The first is to be inspired by the romance of the story and surrender to go forward into the fray because of the adventure of it. The second is to respond with cautious appreciation. To step back and say, "That's an amazing life, but that is not for me. God would have to put a clear calling on my life for me to go do that!" I believe the second response would describe someone like Timothy.

It was Timothy's sense of duty to obey Christ's command that was the foundation of his decision to go with Paul. Although he may have felt underqualified and ill-equipped for the task, he surrendered to go to the uttermost because he knew Christ would honor his obedience.

Timothy traveled the world with Paul until he ended up in Crete. He didn't have any assurances of where the road would take him or even if the journey was safe. As a disciple of Christ, he knew he had a calling to take the gospel to every creature; and Paul's prodding was all he needed to get going.

Timothy had the mind of Christ. He was humble, willing to serve and ready to go. He was surrendered to the unknown. He was surrendered to the difficult reality of missionary life. I believe that it was not until Timothy launched out with the Apostle Paul that he came to fully understand his calling. In 1 Timothy 4:14 Paul writes, "Neglect not the gift that is in thee, which was given thee by prophecy, with the laying on of the hands of the presbytery."

Timid Timothy choose to follow the Apostle Paul to the uttermost. As a result, the Spirit of God equipped him for the task to which he surrendered. He surrendered to the next step.

If you are like Paul, chances are you have a good idea of where you will be going and what you will be doing with your life. Maybe you fit the John Mark type and need more preparation for the harsh reality of the unknown. Or maybe you are a Timothy who is ready and willing to go but needs the prodding of a veteran or visionary leader. Whatever your personality, God has a plan and a place for you. The best way to find your *where* in the call to go is to ask God to not only use you but seek to find where God is at work and ask Him if you can join Him there. I am not seeking what I can do for God as much as I am seeking to know what God is doing in this world and pursuing partnership with Him, even if it means going to the uttermost part of the earth.

For we are labourers together with God...

I Corinthians 3:9

Now I say that Jesus Christ was a minister of the circumcision for the truth of God, to confirm the promises *made* unto the fathers: And that the Gentiles might glorify God for *his* mercy; as it is written, For this cause I will confess to thee among the Gentiles, and sing unto thy name. And again he saith, Rejoice, ye Gentiles, with his people. And again, Praise the Lord, all ye Gentiles; and laud him, all ye people. And again, Esaias saith, There shall be a root of Jesse, and he that shall rise to reign over the Gentiles; in him shall the Gentiles trust. Now the God of hope fill you with all joy and peace in believing, that ye may abound in hope, through the power of the Holy Ghost. And I myself also am persuaded of you, my brethren, that ye also are full of goodness, filled with all knowledge, able also to admonish one another. Nevertheless, brethren, I have written the more boldly unto you in some sort, as putting you in mind, because of the grace that is given to me of God, That I should be the minister of Jesus Christ to the Gentiles, ministering the gospel of God, that the offering up of the Gentiles might be acceptable, being sanctified by the Holy Ghost. I have therefore whereof I may glory through Jesus Christ in those things which pertain to God. For I will not dare to speak of any of those things which Christ hath not wrought by me, to make the Gentiles obedient, by word and deed, Through mighty signs and wonders, by the power of the Spirit of God; so that from Jerusalem, and round about unto Illyricum, I have fully preached the gospel of Christ. Yea, so have I strived to preach the gospel, not where Christ was named, lest I should build upon another man's foundation: But as it is written, To whom he was not spoken of, they shall see: and they that have not heard shall understand. For which cause also I have been much hindered from coming to you. But now having no more place in these parts, and having a great desire these many years to come unto you; Whensoever I take my journey into Spain, I will come to you: for I trust to see you in my journey, and to be brought on my way thitherward by you, if first I be somewhat filled with your *company.*

(Rom 15:8-24)

PART THREE: The Sahara Initiative

What is The Sahara Initiative?

The Sahara Initiative is a project that began in the late 60's and early 70's in which Baptist International Missions, Inc. sought to recruit missionaries for North Africa. The goal was to send missionaries across North Africa to establish gospel preaching centers and plant local churches. Several men and women surrendered to go, and churches were established in countries such as Senegal and Niger. Most of those original missionaries have retired or moved to other fields of service. As it stands, BIMI has only two missionary families serving in North Africa. It is crucial that God sends more laborers to continue the work that has already been established, as well as to launch out unto the uttermost and reach those areas still untouched with the gospel witness.

BIMI is relaunching the Sahara Initiative to reemphasize the opportunities and needs of North Africa. We are specifically praying that God will call twelve missionaries to serve in North Africa. Besides raising awareness of the need and presenting the opportunity to potential recruits, the Sahara Initiative will partner with current missionaries serving in North Africa to provide a missionary internship program focused on preparing missionary candidates for service among the people groups of the Sahara Desert.

First Initiative: Raising Awareness of the Need in the Sahara

If you have attended a mission conference at any mission-minded church, then you have probably heard the phrase "The 10/40 Window." The 10/40 Window is the area approximately between 10 degrees north and 40 degrees north latitude and includes countries located in North Africa, the Middle East and Asia. The 10/40 Window is often called "The Resistant Belt" and includes most of the world's Muslims, Hindus, and Buddhists. More than 5 billion individuals residing in approximately 8,633 distinct people groups can be found in the 10/40 Window. 5,935 (68.7%) of these people groups are considered unreached and have a population of 3.05 billion. This means approximately 61% of the individuals in the 10/40 Window live in an unreached people group. The 10/40 Window is home to some of the largest unreached people groups in the world.

Shortly after Islam was founded, Muslims began a conquest of the Maghreb, swiping across North Africa, razing churches and forcing the submission of tribes to Islam by threat of sword or slavery. Since the 7th century, Islam holds an overpowering stranglehold on the people of North Africa. From governments punishing those who convert from Islam to Christianity with death to threatening shame and banishment in the more democratic nations, Africans living in North Africa have historically had little to no interest in the gospel. I once shared a Bible story with a group of twelve-year-old children who, upon hearing the mention of the name of Jesus, plugged their ears and began chanting, "God has no son, God has no son!" Children are taught from an early age to never read the Bible and never listen to a Christian.

But the resistance to the gospel is beginning to weaken. Modern tools, such as satellite television, the internet, and Smart Phones have given the opportunity for the gospel to reach these unreached people. Men and women from across North Africa are beginning to respond to the message of the love and sacrifice of Jesus Christ.

However, it is one thing to reach people through the airwaves. Thank God for the response to the gospel and for these opportunities to share the gospel. But what North Africa truly needs are men and women who are willing to put feet on the ground and disciple these converts face to face. We need preachers who are willing to pioneer the gospel to one of the hundreds of unreached people groups throughout North Africa. We need men and women to surrender to go to the Sahara and labor for what may be a lifetime to bring the gospel to those who have never heard. North Africa needs church-planters.

Second Initiative: Strategic Church Planting throughout the Sahara

Planting local, indigenous, evangelistic churches is the only solution for meeting the spiritual and physical needs of the world. Not only does the gospel bring the hope of eternal life, but the community it creates in the body of Christ becomes an efficient system of support and development. Paul wrote to the Galatian church that we are to bear one another's burdens. In Romans 15:1, we read, "We then that are strong ought to bear the infirmities of the weak, and not to please ourselves." Only the local church can meet all the needs (both spiritual and physical) of man through the preaching and practice of the gospel. The greatest need in missions today is for church-planting preachers. The nations need the local church. They do not need more social aid or religion. They need the gospel. They need gospel preaching local churches. The world needs Christ.

The Biblical mandate to preach the gospel in all the world was given to the church. The individual missionary is not the solution to man's greatest need. The missionary is simply an instrument through whom God works to bring about the fulfillment of His plan. God's plan is that local churches be established among all nations. The world does not need short-termers or ill-prepared missionaries who leave after their first term on the field. The world needs missionaries who are determined to plant themselves in a desolate region without an established church and stay there until a church is born. The result of the gospel being preached, and disciples being formed is the establishment of local churches. Sometimes this process takes a year or two. Sometimes it takes a lifetime of sacrifice.

Paul knew that the most effective way to reach a people group in a region was to establish local churches. He wrote the church at Thessalonica, declaring, "For from you sounded out the word of the Lord not only in Macedonia and Achaia, but also in every place your faith to God-ward is spread abroad; so that we need not to speak any thing" (1 Thessalonians 1:8). A local church on fire for Christ makes the individual missionary obsolete. That is a good thing! Paul said that his job was done; he was no longer needed because they were sounding forth the word of the Lord in all the region. He was free to move on to the next unreached region. Establishing local churches is the most effective way to reach a region with the gospel. North Africa needs churches and missionaries who will come determined to stay until churches are established.

Third Initiative: Preparing the Called for Ministry in the Sahara

In December of 2005, my wife and I were officially approved to serve with Baptist International Missions, Inc. We were newlyweds, and I was not six months graduated from Bible college. My pastor at the time was on the board of BIMI. After being approved, another board member expressed concern to my pastor about my young age, asking, "Does Josh have any practical experience?" At the time, I was an intern at my local church in rural Michigan.

I thought about his question. What practical experience can someone going to Africa receive while serving in a farming community in Midwest America? I had taken a month-long mission trip to Senegal, but that in no way could prepare me with practical experience for long-term service. I

115

asked myself, "What if there were a program that allowed a missionary or a missionary couple to intern on the mission field for an extended period without needing to raise full support first?" From this seed-thought grew the concept of the need for a missionary internship program. A short-term mission trip is not designed to prepare a missionary candidate for long-term effective service.

Every year, over 2 million Americans go on a short-term mission trips, making it a 2.4 billion dollars per year industry. There is debate in the missionary community about whether short-term mission trips hurt or help the work of missions. I am very supportive of short-term mission trips, when they are done right. But we are facing a major crisis in the missionary work force to the point that many mission agencies are becoming dependent upon short-termers to carry the work on the field. This is not sustainable in the long run.

Charity work and financial aid alone are not enough. In his book *Toxic Charity*, Robert Lupton writes, "Contrary to popular belief, most mission trips and service projects do not: empower those being served, engender healthy cross-cultural relationships, improve quality of life, relieve poverty, change the lives of participants [or] increase support for long-term missions work." Quoting stats from the same book, Darren Carson, founder of Teaching Leaders International, notes the hard reality that charities and short-term aid work has failed Africa. He reveals that over the past fifty years, Africa has received 1 trillion dollars in benevolent aid, but the per capita income is lower, adult literacy rate is lower, and the life expectancy rate has stagnated.[4]

Charity and non-profit organizations, while they serve an important role, especially in developing countries, cannot meet the true need of every society. Neither are they the most efficient means of caring for the poor. 85% of aid money never reaches the targeted areas of need. The singer Bono has recently been under fire when it was discovered that only 1% of money given to his charity ONE actually reaches the needy![5]

While the financial development of poverty-stricken countries and social justice work might fall under the broader category of mission trips, we are concerned primarily with the fulfillment of the Great Commission. Often, short-term mission trips are more for the benefit of those taking the trip rather than for the people to whom they are ministering. I love

---

[4]Carson, Darren (2012, June 10) Why You Should Consider Canceling Your Short-Term Mission Trips. Retrieved May 18, 2018. www.thegospelcoalition.org

[5]Daily Mail Reporter. (2010, 23 September) Bono's ONE foundation under fire for giving little over 1% of funds to charity. Retrieved from http://www.dailymail.co.uk

short-term mission trips because of the impact it has on those who are willing to go. Many have returned to the States having had their worldview either challenged or broadened. There are many men and women who have been called or have confirmed their calling to a mission field on a mission trip. Many laymen who have visited Senegal returned to their home determined to become more involved in giving to missions and reaching the lost in their hometown. Short-term mission trips may help raise awareness of the need in North Africa, but what we need are full-time missionaries who are committed to spending a career sharing the gospel and planting churches in this region of the world.

Serving in North Africa is not an easy task. A mission director once told me that the reason so few go to this part of the 10/40 window is not primarily because we are unaware of the need. That is certainly a contributing factor. However, almost every mission conference speaker will refer to the 10/40 window at some point in his sermon. We know the 10/40 window needs preachers! The director explained that the reason so few go to this region of the world is that it is hard, it is expensive, and it is dangerous. The Next Step: North Africa Missionary Internship is a year-long intensive internship program which will prepare the missionary candidate for the hardship and challenges he or she will face serving in North Africa.

The Next Step: North Africa Missionary Internship is not a short-term mission trip in the traditional sense. The primary objective of a short-term mission trip is to assist a missionary in a specific ministry, such as a building project or mass evangelism effort. The objective of The Next Step: North Africa Missionary Internship is to prepare the intern for effective, long-term ministry, particularly across North Africa.

- A short-term mission trip can confirm God's call to missions in your life. The Next Step: North Africa Missionary Internship is targeted to those who have already confirmed God's call to mission work.

- A short-term trip is an investment in the missionary on the field and his work. The Next Step Internship is an investment in the future ministry of the intern.

- A short-term trip is temporary with an end in sight. The Next Step: North Africa Missionary Internship program is only the beginning of a missionary career. The Next Step: North Africa Missionary Internship is about preparation and longevity. We believe that effective preparation is essential to longevity on the mission field. The better you prepare, the longer you will endure.

The Next Step: North Africa Missionary Internship is not a survey trip. The goal of a survey trip is to outline the details concerning where you will be serving and in what capacity. A survey trip is essential to answer questions such as, Will I serve in a city or village? What languages do I learn and where do I learn them? What does it cost to rent, to buy a car and groceries? Is there electricity? Do I ship a container or are materials readily available in the country? You get the picture. Survey trips answer targeted questions about the daily ins and outs of what life will be like in the country.

Even if you found the answer to every question you asked on your survey trip, you are still lacking one essential element that both determines and proves your readiness: experience. The experience of actually living out the answers to those questions cannot be addressed on a survey trip. It is one thing to find out from where you will purchase your groceries in country. It is an entirely different thing to go to the market, find a fresh cut of meat not covered with too many flies and then barter to get the price down enough so that you are at least not paying double what a national would pay. *The experience of these questions, not the answers themselves is what induces culture shock.* Culture shock contributes greatly to the missionary attrition rate. Spending an extended time on the mission field before you raise full support will help inoculate you to the effects of culture shock.

Survey trips are highly recommended, and several great resources and books are available to the missionary who has reached this stage. Again, the point of this book is not to outline how to take an effective survey trip. I simply want to state that The Next Step internship program is not a survey trip. Where a survey trip offers answers, The Next Step offers the experience to the questions you have about missions and missionary life. I believe that a missionary candidate who successfully completes The Next Step program will be better prepared not only for long-term mission work but also to take a more effective survey trip.

What is The Next Step: North Africa Missionary Internship? Very simply, it is an intensive, real-life training opportunity that will better prepare the missionary candidate for long-term effectiveness on a difficult mission field. The Next Step Internship program offers a strategic approach to preparing a young couple or single missionary candidate for full-time service on the mission field. Preparedness requires us to face reality head-on. Candidates for the mission field need to know what they are getting into before they leave for the field. I know several who raised full support, moved their family overseas and after a couple years of service, returned home because they faced cultural difficulties they had not expected. Ignorant expectations are just as harmful as false expectations. We need to know what we are getting into and learn to persevere early on in our work as missionaries. This is a hard lesson to learn late in your ministry career.

To better prepare a candidate for ministry in North Africa, we have developed a few steps that a participant in the program will take:

1. **Develop the dynamic of your relationship with your sending church**

   - Establishing a temporary base, the candidate will prepare to raise funds for his participation in the program by working from and serving in his sending church.

   - The importance of a healthy relationship between the sent one and the sender cannot be stressed enough. The relationship a missionary has with his sending and supporting churches is even more important than the one he has to his mission agency.

- A healthy relationship with the sending church is essential to a missionary's longevity on the field.

- Serving in the sending church for a short period prior to going will also allow the church leadership to evaluate the candidate's readiness.

2. Attend Camp BIMI

- The prospective intern will attend a week of Camp BIMI at the headquarters of Baptist International Missions, Inc near Chattanooga, Tennessee.

- Camp BIMI will help prepare the candidate mentally as well as spiritually for the challenges of the mission field.

- Spending a week at Camp BIMI will help him to better comprehend the experiences and challenges that will be faced during the one-year internship on the field.

- The week spent at Camp BIMI will help the candidate to learn how to internalize experiences on the field in real time in order to maximize his or her preparation and training.

- Camp BIMI will help the candidate better articulate to supporting churches his mission and his needs.

- No soldier is sent to basic training until he is first challenged in mind, body, and spirit at boot camp. Camp BIMI is like boot camp, only without the physical challenge of a military boot camp, of course!

3. **Go through a screening process to be approved for The Sahara Initiative internship fund**

- The Next Step intern will meet with the BIMI Africa Director to be evaluated and approved for the Next Step Internship program.

- Every missionary candidate who applies to The Next Step: North Africa Missionary Internship program must go through a screening process. We are serious when we say that The Next Step: North Africa Missionary Internship is not a short-term missions trip. We are looking for serious missionary candidates who know they are called to mission work.

- The approval of the director does not make you an official BIMI missionary.

- The purpose of the meeting is to screen the candidates on behalf of the missionary on the field as well as to approve access to The Sahara Internship funds.

- The Next Step: North Africa Missionary Internship is not for someone who is looking to take an extended mission trip because they think it would enrich their life experience. The Next Step: North Africa Missionary Internship is for the man, woman, or couple who knows a true call to full-time missions.

- The Sahara Initiative internship fund is a fund that is supported by churches across North America who have partnered with BIMI to help better prepare missionary candidates.

- This fund is available to cover the ministry

expenses of the candidate while on the field and *goes directly to the BIMI missionary with whom he is working.*

- The candidate who is approved by the committee will need to raise only about 20% of the incurred expenses for living on the field for a year.

4. Step into "mini-deputation"

- Having completed one week of Camp BIMI, the candidate will return to his sending church and begin raising personal support.

- The candidate will receive an information packet as well as promotional materials to assist him in raising support.

- The amount needed to be raised will be determined by the missionary with whom he will work and will cover basic living costs.

- This "mini-deputation" will give important practical experience to help the candidate become more effective in future deputation ministry.

- Although the amount of funds needed to be raised is minimal, the process of this "mini-deputation" will help both the missionary candidate and the sending church better prepare for the challenges of deputation.

5. Step onto the mission field

- Upon raising personal support, the candidate will move to the field and immediately begin language acquisition and cultural training.

- He will be strategically placed into real-life everyday living situations that will help better prepare him for a long-term career. It is easy to be blinded to the reality and even the drudgery of missionary life on a short-term mission trip. Our goal is to push the candidate's limits to the point where he is relying solely on the call of God and not the romance of the field to keep him there.

6. Step into real life ministry

- During the year internship, a candidate will experience real-life ministry through personal involvement in the various outreach programs of the church plant. In Senegal we minister to a predominantly Muslim population. We have developed several ministries targeted at our specific demographic.

- As an intern, you will have an opportunity to plug into the various ministries of the church plant, from teaching English to media outreach to preaching and teaching.

- Where English is not the primary spoken language, you will work to develop a second language with a language partner.

Is a Missionary Internship Program Like This Necessary?

We have been asked, "Why not just raise full support and learn these experiences during your first term?" This is a legitimate question. It is true that currently this is how the vast majority of missionaries learn to handle life on the mission field. Unfortunately, the shock of facing these unexpected real-life situations often contributes heavily to a missionary's decision to leave the field. A missionary who has raised full support experiences a level of internal pressure that he must meet the unspoken expectations of his supporters. I say it is unspoken because most supporting churches do not put this pressure on the missionary. The pressure to meet expectations of results is usually a stress the missionary puts on himself, *especially* because he has full support.

The candidate who has not yet raised full support does not have the same self-inflicted pressure to perform. Without the added burden, the missionary intern is freer to express his feelings of inadequacy and work toward reconciling his own expectations with actual results, and in turn grow in development. When a missionary is free to focus on understanding his sufficiency in Christ, not on what he supposes his supporters will think of him, he is free to grow into effective usefulness.

If the experience of real-life missions proves to be too much and the intern missionary goes home, from a purely financial standpoint, there is a lesser impact than if a fully supported missionary were to leave the field. However, the purpose of The Next Step: North Africa Missionary Internship program is not primarily financial. I believe it is a spiritual preparation that will help reduce the attrition rate in missionaries who would likely burn out trying to learn the reality of mission life and facing culture shock while at the same time reporting something positive every other month to their supporters.

Step Into Your calling

Upon completion of the program, the intern will return home and give an update to his sending church. He would then be ready to begin the process of raising full support. Having survived an intensive year on the field, he will be better equipped to communicate to prospective supporting churches both his passion and his vision. He will also have a broader network of churches who support The Sahara Initiative from which to contact when he begins raising support. A church that is familiar with The Next Step: North Africa Missionary Internship or the Sahara Initiative will be confident in the consideration of supporting a missionary candidate who has completed the program.

An Unfinished Task

The Apostle John was given a tour of heaven in a vision. He was overwhelmed with the sights and sounds. He was overcome with the awe of the presence of God and the sight of the vast multitude worshiping before His throne. In Revelation 5:9-14, John describes what he sees as the Lamb takes the scroll from the One seated on the throne.

> "And they sung a new song, saying, Thou art worthy to take the book, and to open the seals thereof: for thou wast slain, and hast redeemed us to God by thy blood out of every kindred, and tongue, and people, and nation; And hast made us unto our God kings and priests: and we shall reign on the earth. And I beheld, and I heard the voice of many angels round about the throne and the beasts and the elders: and the number of them was ten thousand times ten thousand, and thousands of thousands; Saying with a loud voice, Worthy is the Lamb that was slain to receive power, and riches, and wisdom, and strength, and honour, and glory, and blessing. And every creature which is in heaven, and on the earth, and under the earth, and such as are in the sea, and all that are in them, heard I saying, Blessing, and honour, and glory, and power, be unto him that sitteth upon the throne, and unto the

Lamb for ever and ever. And the four beasts said, Amen. And the four and twenty elders fell down and worshipped him that liveth for ever and ever."

This passage of Scripture describes what the Great Commission looks like in its fulfillment. The Great Commission is all about the glory of God. It is about worship. There is no higher calling. We are commanded to take the gospel to every nation. At the culmination of the ages, God will gather together all things in Christ. The Lamb has been slain and has all authority over the affairs of men. He will rule and reign on earth. All will submit to the Lamb; every knee will bow, and every tongue will confess. Only the individuals who confess Christ while living on earth will join this scene of worship before the throne.

Those who do not receive Christ in this life will confess Him in the next but will not receive salvation. We are commanded to go to every ethnicity, every nation, and every kindred and preach the gospel. Paul told Timothy that we are called to instruct those that "oppose themselves; if God peradventure will give them repentance to the acknowledging of the truth" (2 Timothy 2:25). The fruit of our labor will be manifested in this great day before the throne when those redeemed from every kindred, tribe, and tongue will worship the Lamb.

As a God-called preacher of the gospel, I am honored that I get to say that I had a small role in making this glorious day a reality for those whom I have led to Christ. But the task is unfinished. How do we know? Because Christ has not yet returned. Jesus said in Matthew 24:14, "This gospel of the kingdom shall be preached in all the world for a witness unto all nations; and then shall the end come." I believe we are nearing the end, and Christ will return soon to gather His church unto himself. But the reason that He has not yet returned is due to the fact that "God is longsuffering to us-ward, not willing that any should perish, but that all should come to repentance" (2 Peter 3:9). Until the Lord returns for his bride, the church has an obligation to take the gospel to every nation, kindred, tribe and tongue.

Plans Change. The Call Remains the Same

God is unchangeable. His gifts are unchanging. His calling is unchanging. Positions in ministry and places of service may change. But at the core of who you are, as a God-called preacher, you have an unchanging obligation to evangelize the unreached. Whether in America or abroad, we must be ever seeking to engage the unreached people groups of our cities and towns with the gospel.

You must not let disappointment and failure discourage you from fulfilling your task. Many things have changed in the course of our ministry. From the moment God confirmed to us His leading to Senegal until the day we set foot in the country, we have been through ups and downs. My college roommate did not finish deputation and is serving the Lord in Canada. The original missionary with whom we had planned to work moved back to the States during our final months of deputation. Even the Paris-Dakar Rally had to be relocated to South America because of the threat of terrorism in North Africa. We were asked if any of these changes would affect our plans to go to Senegal. The answer was no.

God's leading did not change. God's calling had not changed and does not change. People change, plans also change, but God remains the same. The Apostle Paul dealt with changes, opposition, and abandonment. When John Mark returned home in the middle of the first missionary journey, Paul may have been discouraged, but he did not give up on his personal calling. He was disappointed by John's decision, but it didn't change his overall ministry objective. Later in his ministry, Paul was blessed to have Epaphroditus serve alongside him (Philippians 2:25-30). But when Epaphroditus became sick and ultimately had to return to Philippi, it did not change Paul's calling. People might let you down, original goals might not flesh out as planned, and even circumstances can, do, and will change. None of this changes God's calling on your life to take the gospel to the uttermost.

It is my prayer that God will use this book to inspire a generation of young men and women to a renewed commitment to fulfilling the unfinished task of the Great Commission. May we, in the power of the Spirit, take the next step, whatever it may be, toward the evangelization of the uttermost to the glory of God and the exaltation of Jesus Christ.

And **he said unto them, Go** ye into all the world and preach the gospel to every creature...

...**and they went** forth, and preached everywhere, the Lord working with them...

Mark 16:15, 20

For more information about the Mead family, you can visit

www.myuttermost.com

or

contact them through email at

missionaryjoshmead@gmail.com

For more information about Baptist International Missions,
Inc. please visit www.bimi.org

For more information about The Next Step: Sahara Initiative
Missionary Internship program or to receive an application
form, contact Joshua Mead at

missionaryjoshmead@gmail.com

or

BIMI's African Director at bimi.africa@gmail.com